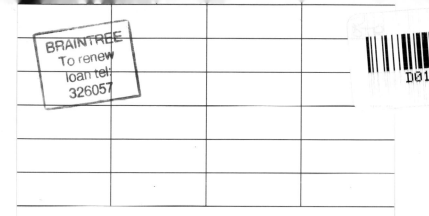

D0190763

This book is to be returned on or before the date above.
It may be borrowed for a further period if not in demand.

**Essex County Council**

# The Lancaster Story

# The Lancaster Story

Peter March

The History Press

Also in this series:

*The Concorde Story*

*The Spitfire Story*

*The Vulcan Story*

*The Red Arrows Story*

*The Harrier Story*

*The Dam Busters Story*

*The Hurricane Story*

*The Lifeboats Story*

*The Stealth Story*

*The SAS Story*

*The Canadian Warplane Heritage's magnificently restored Lancaster 'KB726' operates from Hamilton, Ontario.*

*RAF Battle of Britain Memorial Flight's Lancaster I PA474, here in the colours of No. 9 Squadron.*

First published in the United Kingdom in 2008 by
The History Press
Cirencester Road · Chalford · Stroud · Gloucestershire
GL6 8PE

British Library Cataloguing in Publication Data
A catalogue record for this book is available from the British Library.

Hardback ISBN 978-0-7509-4760-2

Typeset in 9.5/14.5pt Syntax.
Typesetting and origination by
The History Press.
Printed and bound in the United Kingdom.

**Essex County Council Libraries**

# CONTENTS

# ACKNOWLEDGEMENTS

Through the summer months the sight and sound of the RAF Battle of Britain Memorial Flight's Avro Lancaster making a flypast or taking part in a UK airshow has become a memorable feature for young and old. The sound of its four Rolls-Royce Merlin engines brings back memories for the older generation of the tremendous contribution that the bomber made to the successful outcome of the Second World War. Younger people see the big warplane as something of a novelty compared with the small fast jets that have the role in the modern RAF. The story of the Lancaster's development, from Roy Chadwick's Manchester to becoming the most successful Second World War British bomber, is well worth recounting. It is made all the more fascinating by the accounts of some of the spectacular missions and

tales of great heroism by Lancaster aircrew. I am grateful to the authors of the many published references that have been used to compile this short narrative.

Once again I am indebted to Brian Strickland for his careful research into both the background text and the many excellent photographs. I have also received editorial assistance from Ben Dunnell and Michael

▲
*BBMF's Lancaster I PA474 in No. 61 Squadron markings as EE176 'Mickey the Moucher'.*

◄◄
*Painted as 'KB726' VR-A following long restoration, the Canadian Lancaster flew again on 11 September 1988.*

J.F. Bowyer. The brochures produced by the Battle of Britain Memorial Flight have provided a rich source of information. Direct help with the supply of photographs has been given by Michael Bowyer, Bill Bushell, Sue Bushell, Richard Caruana, Jonathan Falconer, Derek James, Terry Lee, Andrew March, Daniel March, Dr Alfred Price, Robby Robinson, Kev Storer, Brian Strickland and Richard L. Ward. The photo files of Avro, Bristol-Siddeley Engines and Rolls-Royce have also produced a number of invaluable photographs.

Peter R. March

➤
*The restored Canadian Lancaster 'KB726' on display in September 2007.*

During the Royal Air Force's expansion programme in the 1930s, heavy bombers had doubled their radius of action and increased their speed by 100mph, as well as doubling their defensive armament and tripling their bomb load. A new generation of high-powered engines, such as the Rolls-Royce Merlin (the RAF's first 1,000hp (740kW) engine) and the Bristol Mercury and Pegasus, were entering production.

At that time, the Air Council made two bold decisions which were to have the most decisive effects on the RAF's operational efficiency in the Second World War. The first was the standardisation of the eight-gun armament for fighters which, with the introduction of radar ground-controlled interception techniques, contributed to their great victory in the Battle of Britain

*Vic formation of Lancaster Is of No. 207 Squadron operating from RAF Bottesford in June 1942.*

▶▶

First prototype Avro Manchester L7246 in its early form with small fins and rudders that first flew on 25 July 1939. The fuselage windows relate to the original trooping requirement.

'As the user of the Lancaster during the last three-and-a-half years of bitter, unrelenting warfare, I would say this to those who placed that shining sword in our hands: "Without your genius and your effort, we would not have prevailed – the Lancaster was the greatest single factor in winning the war".'

Marshal of the Royal Air Force Sir Arthur T. Harris Bt GCB OBE AFC LLD, Air Officer Commanding-in-Chief, Bomber Command February 1942–September 1945.

(see *The Spitfire Story* and *The Hurricane Story* in this series). The second was the decision to proceed with the development of four-engined heavy bombers, armed with power-operated gun turrets. This led to the production of the Short Stirling, Handley Page Halifax and, ultimately, the Avro Type 683 Lancaster.

The Lancaster was probably the most famous, and certainly the most successful, heavy bomber flown by Bomber Command in the Second World War. It was the last of the four-engined bombers to enter operational service, but by the beginning of 1944 it had established its superiority over its rivals. By early 1945, there were no fewer than fifty-six squadrons of Lancasters in front-line service with RAF Bomber Command. No other aircraft accomplished any better the role for which it was

designed. It has often been described as the greatest single factor in winning the Second World War – possibly an exaggeration, but a pardonable one.

The Lancaster owed its origins to the Air Ministry Specification B.12/36 for a twin-engined medium bomber, to be fitted with the new high-powered Rolls-Royce X-type Vulture 24-cylinder engine of 1,760hp (1,306kW). The first aircraft built to this specification was the Avro 679 Manchester, the prototype of which first flew on 25 July 1939. Some eighteen months later, in November 1940, the Manchester began to go into squadron service with the RAF. No. 207 Squadron of Bomber Command was the first to be equipped with the Manchester I, but the aircraft suffered terribly from poor engine performance and shocking engine reliability. One unit, No. 97 Squadron, was grounded so often that it was nicknamed 'the 97th Foot'. The Vulture engine was unable to produce the specified power and was so complicated, with four banks of cylinders all feeding the same crankshaft, that it never achieved any sort of reliability. There were two projects for remedying the shortcomings: replacing the Vultures with two Napier Sabre or two Bristol Centaurus engines, or using four engines.

The design by Avro of a four-Merlin version of the Manchester had actually commenced early in 1939, using the Merlin X as its basis. This engine was already proven in the Spitfire, Hurricane and Whitley. The Merlin X had just been designed for the Bristol Beaufighter II, in the form of a self-contained unit that could be bolted on and coupled up without the need for any design effort by Avro, beyond increasing yet again the span of the outer wings. The design was nearly complete in 1940. However, an official decision on this design was delayed because of the large demands on supply of the Merlin engine for fighter production. Nonetheless, owing to hold-ups in the development of the Vulture engine and overheating problems with those in service, the decision was taken in mid-1940 to continue with the design of a new variant of the Manchester, to be fitted with four Merlins.

◄
*Manchester L7515 of No. 207 Squadron at RAF Bottesford, one of the last to be delivered.*

**Did you know?**
It took nearly 10 tonnes of light aluminium alloy to make each Lancaster, and a six-month production period at peak would require sufficient light alloy sheet to cover a roadway 31ft wide and stretching between the Manchester factory of A.V. Roe and London.

In August 1940, Air Chief Marshal Sir Charles Portal, Chief of the Air Staff, authorised immediate efforts to introduce four-engined heavy bombers into service as quickly as possible. Somewhat surprisingly, Avro was asked to switch to production of the Handley Page HP57 Halifax. This request was strongly resisted by the manufacturer as it was pointed out that, with two Manchester assembly lines in operation, it would be much simpler to introduce its four-engined version into those lines, once the prototype had confirmed the viability of the larger bomber. Fortunately, this view was accepted by the Air Staff in September 1940. Two prototypes were therefore ordered and accorded maximum priority.

The first conversion made use of about 75 per cent of Manchester parts and assemblies, the principal changes being

the new centre-section with mountings for four Merlin engines. This aircraft became the first prototype of the Lancaster. A second prototype fitted with four Merlin XX engines, and considerably modified in detail, was designed, built and flown within eight months. But without the Manchester, there would have been no Lancaster.

Apart from fabric-covered ailerons, the Lancaster I was of all-metal construction and was built in subsections to facilitate production and final assembly. The Lancaster proved an excellent production design, readily suited to divided manufacture by, eventually, five major UK contractors in seven separate towns. Peak production by one major manufacturer rose to 155 aircraft in one month during 1944. The fuselage and wings, each in five sections, were made of light alloys bolted together

**Did you know?**
About 10,500 individual drawings were used for the construction of a Lancaster.

7

➤
*The second of the three Lancaster prototypes, DG595 with four Merlin Xs. It first flew on 13 May 1941.*

**Did you know?**

The Lancaster, regarded by many as the greatest bomber of the Second World War, was borne out of the failed Avro Manchester.

in the final assembly. The only sections of the bomber covered in fabric were the 17ft-long ailerons. Finally, over 600 sub-contractors were involved in component manufacture.

The prototype (BT308), which initially featured a triple-fin design and was widely known as the Manchester III, took to the air from the Avro factory airfield at Woodford near Stockport on 9 January 1941. Some eighteen days after this first flight, the prototype was delivered to the Aeroplane and Armament Experimental Establishment (A&AEE) at RAF Boscombe Down, where it received the best assessment ever awarded to a new aircraft, beginning: 'This aircraft is eminently suitable for operational service.' Following early handling trials it was suggested that the bomber be fitted with larger twin fins and that the central fin be removed. It received favourable reports as to its handling and especially its speed, a maximum of 310mph (499km/h) at 21,000ft (6,401m) being recorded.

After the trials, BT308 visited some of the operational squadrons which would soon be operating the new bomber. It was then delivered to Rolls-Royce for exhaust flame damping trials in early 1942, and then to the Royal Aircraft Establishment (RAE) at Farnborough for trials with the

Metropolitan-Vickers F.2 turbojet, which was installed in the tail. It was struck off charge in May 1944.

The first production Lancaster, L7527, flew on 31 October 1941, with 1,280hp (955kW) Merlin XX engines in place of the 1,145hp (854kW) Merlin Xs used previously.

'Its vertical banks, long sustained climbs at a steep angle and remarkably small turning circle are proof of its magnificent handling qualities. These impressions are reinforced when flying and performing. In fact, the Lancaster, despite its size, is one of the sweetest aeroplanes on the controls yet built. The ailerons in particular are extremely light and positive.'

Capt Bill Thorn, Avro's deputy chief test pilot, during the Second World War.

Production deliveries commenced later in the year. The first unit to receive the Lancaster was No. 44 (Rhodesia) Squadron at RAF Waddington, for general evaluation and crew training, when it took on three aircraft on Christmas Eve 1941. The unit went into battle with its Lancaster Is early in 1942 and the new bomber was well received by its crews. Early Lancasters retained the Manchester's FN.21A two-gun ventral turret, but this was rarely used and soon discarded. This was a disastrous decision, as later this was the only turret that could have done any good in combat with German night fighters.

The cycle of raids intensified still further through that year, with deliveries of the new bomber to other squadrons of Bomber Command. Canadian-built Lancasters, which were of commendable quality,

**Did you know?**
A normal 'tour' of operations was 30 sorties, after which a crew got a spell out of the front line, perhaps instructing new aircrew. But the average operational life was just 14 sorties for Bomber Command aircraft, and the odds on you actually finishing a tour were typically 7:1 against.

commenced delivery by air across the Atlantic in September 1943. With increased Lancaster production, No. 5 Group was formed, entirely equipped with the type.

It was by far the most important instrument of Air Chief Marshal 'Bomber' Harris's policy of night attacks on German cities. The Lancaster was in service just in time to participate in the first 'Thousand-Bomber Raid' on the night of 30/31 May 1942.

Lancasters not only made the biggest contribution to Bomber Command's night offensive on Germany, but they also helped to turn the scale in the great land battles of 1944 by bombing German armies in the field.

A total of 7,377 Lancasters were built. The type flew 156,318 sorties, dropped 608,613 tons of bombs and laid a substantial number of sea mines. However, 3,345 were lost in action, involving the loss of 21,751 crew members, killed or missing.

Out of a compromise, and expected at best to be slightly inferior from the outset, the Lancaster became Bomber Command's most potent heavy asset of the war. The supremacy of the four-engined Avro design in later years showed what an excellent compromise the aircraft had proved to be, and a tribute to the soundness of the basic design and structure.

With the departure of B-17 Flying Fortresses and B-24 Liberators, supplied under Lend-Lease, from the RAF in 1945, the Lancaster became Coastal Command's main land-based maritime reconnaissance aircraft, until finally being replaced by the interim Lockheed Neptune and then the Avro Shackleton in early 1954.

The Lancaster was brought into service in less time from prototype to service stage than any other RAF bomber. Its first operational use came on 3 March 1942, when four aircraft from No. 44 Squadron successfully laid mines in Heligoland Bight. This was referred to as 'gardening' – the invariable operational term for 'laying mines in enemy water'. All returned safely – the Lancaster was operational. The first bombing raid occurred on 10 March, when two aircraft from No. 44 Squadron each took 5,050lb (2,291kg) of incendiaries to Essen. On 21 March the second Lancaster squadron undertook its first operation.

Two squadrons were tasked with a daring and dangerous long-distance, low-level raid in daylight on 17 April 1942, to destroy the MAN factory at Augsburg that was manufacturing diesel engines for U-boats. Nos 44 and 97 Squadrons were detailed to provide six Lancasters each for the mission. Of the twelve aircraft that departed Lincolnshire, only five returned. Squadron Leader Nettleton, the CO of No. 44 Squadron was awarded the Victoria Cross (the first of ten to go to Lancaster crew members) for his courage and leadership. The mission caused considerable disruption to production at Augsburg, but in addition it

*Lancaster 1 R5689 VN-N of No. 50 Squadron at RAF Swinderby in August 1942.*

A No. 75 Squadron RNZAF aircraft undergoing maintenance at RAF Mepal.

**Did you know?**
It was to be by virtue of a spectacular low-level daylight raid by twelve aircraft from both Nos 44 and 97 Squadrons on Augsburg on 7 April 1942 that the Lancaster first made the newspaper headlines.

threw the Lancaster into the consciousness of the British public. The reason for this extraordinary mission was never explained and it was never repeated.

Throughout the remainder of 1942, the Lancaster was an immediate success and the numbers made available gradually increased. By the end of the year, No. 5

Group was equipped with nine units. Some Lancasters carried 'second dickey' pilots, to give them operational experience before their first mission in command. A pilot's first introduction to the type in Bomber Command was usually at a Lancaster Finishing School (LFS), most aircraft being ex-operational. The new pilot, straight

◄

*Lancaster II DS604/OR-W carries the markings of No. 61 Squadron at RAF Syerston in this late 1942 picture. The following year the aircraft was passed to No. 45 Squadron at East Wreatham when No. 61 standardised on the MkI/III. Coded KO-B it was posted missing after a mission to Frankfurt on the night of 10/11 April 1943.*

**Did you know?**

The Lancaster's normal crew was seven comprising pilot, flight engineer, navigator, wireless operator, rear gunner, mid-upper gunner and bomb aimer (who also manned the front turret).

➤

*Crews of No. 103 Squadron at RAF Elsham Wolds sitting on bombs about to loaded on ED888 PM-M2, and watching additional nose art being applied to the bomber.*

from the conversion unit, was taken off for a circuit or two in a dual Lancaster and then launched with his crew. There was power to spare and the brakes worked well.

A Lancaster aircrew's average age was 23, and most were a mixture of officers and NCOs. The pilot was the captain of the aircraft, regardless of rank – and rank mattered not all that much in the wartime Bomber Command. Crews were a mix of nationalities, with many Canadians, Aussies, New Zealanders, Poles and even some

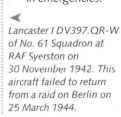

*Lancaster I DV397.QR-W of No. 61 Squadron at RAF Syerston on 30 November 1942. This aircraft failed to return from a raid on Berlin on 25 March 1944.*

Americans. Many months of individual training on smaller and simpler aircraft preceded a crew being welded together into an efficient team at an operational training unit.

The Lancaster was designed to be flown by a single pilot, though a single sortie could last as long as 10 hours, as in the spring of 1942 the second pilot was considered superfluous. However, a new and important crew member was introduced: the flight engineer. The captain sat up straight in a tall seat high as a throne – its high steel back was the only piece of armour plate in the entire aircraft. There was no co-pilot as such, so a 9-hour zig-zag flight across Europe to eastern Germany (such as the raid on Berlin, the first since 1941, by an all-Lancaster force on 16 January 1943) called for considerable physical endurance from all, particularly the pilot. The flight engineer sat behind the pilot, facing his systems panel on the fuselage's starboard wall, and was trained by the pilot to fly the aircraft straight and level. The navigator had a curtained-off cubicle behind with his charts and clumsy Dalton navigational computer, and 'Sparks', the wireless operator, had little contact with the outside world once ensconced in their offices, together with the three gunners. The normal seven-man crew was on some occasions supplemented by an eighth, an extra 'Sparks' to operate jamming equipment or radio countermeasures. In some Pathfinder aircraft there could be an extra navigator to work the $H_2S$ (a radio-navigation aid) to exacting standards. The rear gunner had the loneliest post, in his power-operated turret with its four 0.303s, out of sight of the rest of the crew and

*Groundcrew refuelling Lancaster BII/EQ-Z Zombie of No. 408 (Goose) Squadron RCAF at RAF Linton-on-Ouse prior to a raid on Cologne on 24 April 1944.*

**Did you know?**

Apart from minor changes such as the gradual filling-in of thirteen small slit windows on each side and the fitting of bulged bomb doors, the Lancaster airframe remained virtually unchanged throughout its life.

*Lancaster III LM446/ PG-H here flying with No. 619 Squadron at RAF Dunholme Lodge. Originally formed at Woodhall Spa the Squadron flew over 3,000 sorties during the Second World War and lost 77 Lancasters.*

*NG361/OJ-E of No. 149 Squadron at RAF Methwold, pictured in January 1945. It was one of a total of 7,373 Lancasters produced during the war.*

only in touch with them via the electric intercom.

Normal fuel capacity was 2,154 gallons (9,792 litres) of 100-octane fuel, and one mile to the gallon was considered good going. Each Merlin needed 37.5 gallons (170 litres) of oil, of which it used between 10–16 pints (5.68–9.1 litres) per hour for normal running. Take-off speed was between 95 and 105mph (153–169km/h), with the port throttles being advanced slightly to counter the swing to port. Initial climbing speed to 12,000ft was 160mph (257km/h) with a rate of climb of 250ft/min. The pilots' notes of the period stated: 'there is good warning of stall with slight tail buffeting; there is no tendency to drop a wing.' A normal landing approach commenced at 132mph (212km/h), passing over the airfield

'The aircraft is eminently suitable for operational duties. The performance and handling characteristics with full load surpass those of any other bomber. Even with two engines stopped on one side the performance is exceptional. Baulked landings present no difficulties even with 60,000lb loaded weight. Take-off and night landing are straightforward. Manoeuvrability is good and evasive tactics easy.'

The late Sir Peter Masefield, wartime Technical Editor of *The Aeroplane*, in August 1942.

boundary fence at 109mph (176km/h). It could fly successfully on any two engines, and when light on one engine, though with reducing altitude. When fully laden, the Lancaster needed a take-off run of between 3,600 and 4,500ft carrying a load equivalent to its own weight of 35,000lb (15,876kg) – by modern standards, a modest performance, but in its day, matched by none.

By 1945, the efficiency and versatility of the Lancaster made RAF Bomber Command almost a 'Lancaster Command'. As of April 1945, out of 1,609 aircraft crews available daily, 1,087 were operational on Lancasters.

Virtually every Lancaster built during the war went to Bomber Command in the UK for the strategic bomber offensive. Only at the end of the war did the first Lancasters move to the Middle East too late to see action there. Apart from a few detachments, Coastal Command's desire for Lancasters remained unfilled until after the end of the bombing campaign.

**Did you know?**
Lancasters took part in almost every major bombing raid of the campaign in Europe from mid-1942 until the end of hostilities.

At first, Lancasters were largely navigated by dead reckoning, and bombing visually aimed. A number of bombing aids were coming into use that were to make the 'heavies' far more effective weapons. Electronic aids subsequently brought greater accuracy: Rebecca, the Gee nav aid, Gee-H (aircraft thus equipped had two horizontal yellow bands on their fins) and on special target-marking missions, Oboe, a radar navigation and blind bombing system which guided the crews to the targets by signals from ground stations. The H$_2$S, which by radar gave a semi-pictorial view

**Did you know?**

Eventually, almost all squadron Lancasters of Bomber Command were equipped with H$_2$S airborne radar scanners.

➤

*No. 15 Squadron at RAF Mildenhall operated this Lancaster NG358/LS-H equipped with Gee-H radar equipment in the latter stages of the war. The yellow G-H tail colours indicate a leader aircraft.*

of the land below housed in a distinctive fat blister under the rear fuselage, was first used on 30 January 1943.

The electronic equipment of the heavies was becoming exceedingly complex and each created its own problem. An important item was the IFF (Identification Friend or Foe), which emitted signals our own defences could receive and identify. This necessitated an aerial – one of the eight aerial systems on a Lancaster – slung from the tip of the fins to the IFF instrument near the mid-turret. A number of Lancasters carried special communications gear in the first electronic countermeasures (ECM) and electronic counter-countermeasures (ECCM) fitments such as the 'Airborne Cigar' radio jammer carried by No. 101 Squadron, whose Lancasters had two large radio masts on top and another projecting down under the nose. Another addition was the Monica radar at the tail to warn off Luftwaffe night-fighters, but this was a disastrous fit as this defence aid was in fact a death-trap, the night-fighters homing in on its emissions.

The raid by Lancasters on Essen on the night of 5–6 March 1943 proved that Oboe was the answer to accurate target location as the intersecting beams placed precisely over the aiming point enabled marking to be carried out effectively, even when the target was obscured by cloud, smoke, industrial haze or a combination of all three.

From 1943 raids saw the first use of a simple radar-jamming device, and brought in their wake the terror of the 'firestorm'. For some time scientists had been working on a method of jamming German ground

**Did you know?**
Only 11 per cent of crews survived being shot down in a Lancaster, while 29 per cent of Halifax aircrew baled out successfully.

Dropping bombs through cloud using H$_2$S on a V1 flying bomb site in northern France on 27 July 1944.

radar, and had in fact come up with a very simple and inexpensive counter-measure which they christened 'Window'. Consisting of strips of aluminium foil, each one measuring 30cm long and 1.5cm wide, Window was dropped in bundles of 2,000 strips held together by an elastic band. As each bundle was released, it formed a cloud of aluminium strips which gave an echo on radar the same size as that received from a Lancaster. Released at one-minute intervals from every Lancaster in the force, Window saturated enemy radar screens to such an extent that controlled interceptions became impossible. This simple device had been perfected in 1942, but its use by Bomber Command was prohibited until such time as British radar, immune to such jamming, had been developed since it was believed that the Germans would soon realise its effectiveness and use it themselves.

The Lancaster settled down to patient slogging, night after night, in ever-larger forces whose techniques improved all the time. Since it proved a very manoeuvrable bomber, an experienced pilot could out-fly a fighter, as many German fighter pilots found to their cost. Throughout the war, the

casualty rate on Lancasters was considerably less than any other bomber type, a feature much appreciated by its crews.

In addition to front-line duties, Lancasters were used for training purposes and eventually there were sixteen Heavy Conversion Units based around the UK. Lancaster VII (FE)s for the proposed Far East operations had improved avionics, including

'Every Lancaster produced is a contribution to victory through the striking power of the air. In congratulating Mr Dobson and Mr Chadwick, their teams, and every man and woman working on the Lancaster, one can honestly say that in it they are producing a war-winning bomber. We cannot have too many Lancasters, and the more there are the quicker the war will be won.'

The late Sir Peter Masefield, wartime Technical Editor of *The Aeroplane*.

◄
*ND991 VN-P of No. 50 Squadron at RAF Skellingthorpe on 10 May 1944 (having made its maiden flight only ten days before) prior to a mission against rail yards at Lille. It survived the war and was later loaned to Flight Refuelling Ltd.*

◄
*To enable more precise bombing in 1943, the Lancaster was fitted with H$_2$S radar and bombing equipment (as here on NG347/QB-P of No. 42 Sqn). The mapping radar in the large blister took up the position of the ventral gun position. By this time the vital Gee navigation aid was also being carried.*

➤
*Ground crews waving to Lancaster ED905 BQ-F of No. 550 Squadron taking off at RAF Killingholme for its 100th operation.*

Gee III, Rebecca II and Loran I to meet American Pacific Theater requirements, and $H_2S$ Mk IIIG.

Like most of the best aircraft, all Lancasters looked almost identical to the first. Apart from special weapon and electronic fits, the only real difference in production machines was the Mk II, which had Bristol Hercules sleeve-valve radial engines. The Mk II had good performance but high fuel consumption, and was used mainly by Canadian crews.

Thanks to the original 1936 specification calling for torpedoes, the Lancaster inherited from the Manchester a gigantic and unobstructed bomb-bay, nearly 33ft (10m) in length. After some strengthening, this was used to carry the heaviest and bulkiest bombs used in the Second World War including the regular 4,000lb (1,184kg) HC (high capacity) 'cookie'.

In general, all Lancasters were fitted to carry up to the 4,000lb bombs. Indeed, most production aircraft from early 1943 onwards could carry 8,000lb bombs. Lancasters able to take the later 12,000lb and 22,000lb giants were classified as 'Specials'. The 4,000lb was the usual weapon carried, while other stores could include eighteen 500lb (227kg) General Purpose bombs for the carpet bombing of tactical targets, surrounded by a dozen or more cases

A very large and unrestricted bomb-bay was inherited from the Manchester and could accommodate the heaviest and bulkiest of the RAF's bombs used in the Second World War.

*An early Lancaster I, L7540/OL-U, flew with No. 83 Squadron at RAF Scampton in June 1942. In the foreground are 4,000lb thin-cased 'cookies' blast bombs. The aircraft's mid-upper turret has not yet received its fairing.*

of incendiaries; the double-length 8,000lb (3,629kg) HC bomb and the rare 12,000lb (5,443kg) Tallboy deep-penetration (DP) streamlined bomb designed by Barnes Wallis, used to sink the *Tirpitz*; the even bigger 22,000lb (9,979kg) Grand Slam DP, only used by Nos 617 and 9 Squadrons, which required substantial aircraft modifications resulting in the designation Mk I (Special); and the special weapon designed by Wallis to breach German dams. Up to six 1,850lb (839kg) parachute mines were carried for mine-laying operations.

All Lancasters could operate at around 22,000ft. This had a distinct advantage as attacks were concentrated with some ten aircraft attacking every minute; the advantage of height made them less prone to being hit by falling bombs, which was the fate of many aircraft.

The early production models, after the deletion of the ventral armament, carried eight 0.303in (7.7mm) Browning machine guns, two each in Frazer Nash FN.5A nose and FN.50 dorsal turrets (which were devoid of fairings on early examples), and four in an FN.20 tail turret. Its capacity was 1,000 rounds per gun.

Most rear turrets eventually had plain apertures cut in the perspex, despite the bitter cold, to give the best view aft. By late 1944, the Lancaster VII came into production with an electrically operated American Martin 250 CE23A dorsal turret containing two 0.50in machine guns instead of the hydraulically operated FN.50 with two 0.303in weapons. The new turret was mounted further forward than its predecessor to a point just aft of the wing's trailing edge.

In some later marks of the Lancaster, the Frazer Nash rear turret with its four Brownings was replaced by a roomier Rose-Rice turret which carried two 0.05in machine guns. The latter enabled the gunner to wear a pilot-type parachute in which the pack was attached to the harness and formed the cushion on which

**Did you know?**

The Lancaster's armament continued more or less standard throughout the war, though the final versions had a different rear turret housing two 0.50in machine guns.

➤
*Armourers loading belts of .303 ammunition to the front turret. The bomb aimer had an optically flat plexiglass panel in the nose cupola through which to sight.*

he sat. Many Lancaster rear gunners owe their lives to this improvement. A few later production aircraft were fitted with a new FN.82 rear turret, also mounting two 0.50in guns. FN.150 and Martin turrets equipped with two 0.50in Brownings were

'The night of 30 March 1944, when I piloted a Lancaster to Nuremberg, is a night I cannot forget because my memory is re-enforced by three basic points. First, this was the night of the big wind and atrocious weather. Second, it was the night when the Lancaster showed qualities which endeared her to all who flew her. For me this was the night when the Lancaster bomber performed the impossible. Third, the question it poses; was this the biggest air defeat of the war?'

Warrant Officer Ken Lane, pilot of
No. 83 (Pathfinder) Squadron Lancaster III
N9333/OL-F, recalling the Nuremberg raid
when ninety-five Lancasters and Halifaxes were lost
in one night.

installed in Canadian-built Mk X aircraft. An F.24 camera was standard equipment for vertical photography to ascertain bombing accuracy.

Some Lancasters used later on by the Pathfinder Force had an Automatic Gun Laying rear turret, known to Bomber Command as 'Village Inn', which

**Did you know?**

No other aircraft of comparable size could take the ever-increasing bomb loads that were required on the Lancaster. Even so, the design was stretched to the limit to accommodate the 22,000lb Grand Slam monster, the ultimate in conventional bombs.

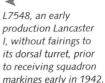

◀

*L7548, an early production Lancaster I, without fairings to its dorsal turret, prior to receiving squadron markings early in 1942.*

automatically sighted and fired at enemy fighters. Only a few such turrets were in service when the war ended, and they were introduced too late to make any difference to the air combat picture.

◄◄
*The Lancaster's mid-upper turret had a fairing for aerodynamic purposes.*

◄
*A late production Lancaster, one of a few delivered with an automatic gun-laying FN121 turret housing a radar sensor. Known to Bomber Command as AGL(T) 'Village Inn' it automatically sighted and fired at an enemy fighter. The aerial above the turret gave warning of an approaching Luftwaffe night fighter using FuG 202/212.*

◄
*A Lancaster rear turret which usually had an open panel in the perspex to give the gunner a better view of marauding German night fighters.*

No account of the Lancaster would be complete without mention of perhaps the most famous raids of the war: the breaching of the Möhne and Eder Dams by No. 617 Squadron, which became known as the 'Dam Busters'. The youngest of the operational squadrons still serving in the RAF, No. 617, is certainly one of the most famous. Its prestige stems almost entirely from a single wartime operation; the extraordinary dams attack of 16–17 May 1943 by Lancasters, led by the legendary Wing Commander Guy Gibson VC. The special bombs resembled giant garden rollers and a requisite was that they had to spin away from the Lancasters. Their bulk necessitated fitting external pylons to the fuselage to take the axle of the bomb, to be revolved before release.

Building on this enviable reputation, No. 617 Squadron and its Lancasters went on to win new laurels in the great bomber offensive of 1943–5. In the postwar years, it was in the forefront of the RAF's advance into the supersonic and nuclear era. Recently, flying Tornados, it has participated in both Iraq conflicts.

The best known of all Lancaster raids in the Second World War was that carried out

▼
*One of the Lancaster BIII (Special) aircraft converted for the Dams Raid in May 1943. This is ED817 AJ/C, that took part in the early test drops but did not participate in the actual attack.*

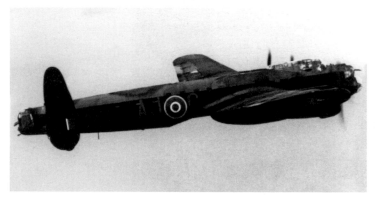

*Wg Cdr Guy Gibson with four of his No. 617 Squadron crew who flew on the Dams Raid. From left to right: Wg Cdr Guy Gibson, Plt Off Fred Spafford, Flt Lt Bob Hutchinson, Plt Off George Dearing and Flg Off Torger Taerum.*

*A modified Lancaster drops a full-size 'Upkeep' off the Kent coast at Reculver Bay, near Margate, in May 1943.*

**Did you know?**

One of the new Lancaster squadrons was No. 106 (formerly a Manchester unit), commanded by a young man who was to stamp his extraordinary qualities of leadership on every operation in which he flew; his name was Wing Commander Guy Gibson DFC.

by No. 617 in 1943 on the german dams in Operation *Chastise*. Dr Barnes N. Wallis had designed a 'bouncing bomb', codenamed Upkeep, with a view to breaching the dams. After much persuasion, Sir Arthur Harris agreed to a special squadron being formed to carry out the operation, as the revolving cylindrical skip bomb weighed 9,000lb and was the heaviest load then carried by a Lancaster. The dorsal turret and bomb-bay doors were removed and the cavities faired over. A drive system was devised to spin the bomb up to the correct launch velocity (approximately 500rpm). The bomb was released while spinning on its longitudinal axis, the backward spin imparting a series of decelerating bounces on the water, so calculated as to enable the mine to come to rest against the dam's parapet before sinking to a predetermined depth, where it would explode against the face of the dam.

◄
*Dambuster's Lancaster flown by No. 617 Squadron's CO, Wg Cdr Guy Gibson, at low level at Reculver in May 1943 during 'Upkeep' trials.*

> Wg Cdr Guy Gibson at
RAF Scampton, together
with some of his crews
and his pet labrador
Nigger that was sadly
killed by a car outside the
main gate on the day of
the Dams Raid.

The Lancasters, using special low-flying techniques, were required to fly at a height of exactly 60ft and release the bomb at 220mph (354km/h). No. 617 Squadron trained at low level around the dams in the UK and twenty special Lancasters were slated for the task. Six dams were listed as targets – the Möhne, Eder and Sorpe, plus three reserves.

On the early evening of 16 May 1943, nineteen Lancasters took off from RAF Scampton and headed out to Germany. The Möhne, the largest dam in Europe, was breached and the next wave attacked the Eder with the same effect. The Sorpe Dam was then damaged. The attack was a great success, causing havoc to the German war machine, while over 1,400 people died on the ground. In the Ruhr, Germany's industrial heartland, coalmines,

'When we were on our way in, we were picked up by searchlights. They were dazzling. The blue light was a master light. Once the blue light was on you, the other ones automatically picked you up. But we were fortunate. We were able to shake it off. But we lost the two aircraft we were going in with. So we carried on singly. As we got down to the Möhne we started down the right side, and the light guns opened up on us. We picked up one hole. Then we joined the other six Lancasters circling the Dam to create confusion and draw a little fire to give the one who was doing the run a better chance. Guy Gibson then called, "This dam's gone", and we were tasked to go for the Eder.'

Danny Walker, Lancaster navigator, No. 617 Squadron.

A Lancaster that was based at RAF Hemswell, Lincolnshire, for the Dambusters film made in the early 1950s.

power stations and factories as far as 40 miles away from the dams were flooded and communications were disrupted over a wide area.

The cost to No. 617 Squadron was high. Of the nineteen aircraft deployed, eight did not return and only three members of the crews of those aircraft survived. Fifty-three crew members were killed. For his outstanding leadership, Wg Cdr Guy Gibson received the Victoria Cross and many of the surviving crew members were also decorated.

Above all, the dams raid gave an immense boost to morale in Britain at that time of the war, and provided the RAF with a massive PR opportunity. The acclaimed film *The Dam Busters* was released in the early 1950s; another movie of the same name is to be made in 2008 in New Zealand using material that was originally classified and has only recently been released.

Throughout the remainder of the war, Bomber Command's Lancasters were operational almost every night, taking the fight to the German nation. The Ruhr, Hamburg, Berlin, Essen, Cologne, Dusseldorf, Nuremburg and many other cities were at the receiving end of consistent, massive Lancaster attacks. Losses were high due to concentrated German flak defences and night fighter action.

Harris approached the Battle of Berlin, a city which he believed could be laid to ruins (given some help by the Americans) by the end of March 1944, without the need to invade Europe. It was felt that a devastated German capital could well persuade the German people to surrender. Berlin was a very different target from Hamburg or the Ruhr, however. It was located well inland and was thus less distinguishable on the bombers' $H_2S$ screens. Also, it was well beyond the range of Oboe and Gee, and the Luftwaffe could be expected to defend it with every day and night fighter available.

The answer apparently lay in the efficiency of Air Vice-Marshal Don Bennett's Lancaster Pathfinders and, not unnaturally, the success of each Berlin raid was directly proportional to the quality of route and target marking by them. In an effort to overcome the Luftwaffe's tactics, a number of innovations were adopted by Bomber Command such as the jamming of enemy broadcast transmitters, and the constant relaying of spurious broadcasts to German pilots. The use of Window continued as a means of confusing the ground radar.

In addition to attacks on cities, raids were also made on important railway interchanges, marshalling yards, canals and oil installations. DP bombs became readily available, and with the newly developed Stabilised Automatic Bomb Sight, premium targets were being hit with outstanding accuracy.

Other great Lancaster feats continued. Using Tallboy bombs, No. 617 Squadron

**Did you know?**

In August 1942, a new Pathfinder Group (No. 8 Group) with Lancasters was created in an attempt to improve the bombing accuracy of Bomber Command.

◄
*No. 83 Squadron at RAF Wyton became a Pathfinder squadron in August 1942 and its Lancasters acted as target markers for the main force of bombers until the German surrender in May 1945.*

made various attempts to sink the German battleship *Tirpitz*, lurking in the Alten Fjord in northern Norway. This required the Lancasters to operate out of Russia for some missions. A final attack on 12 November 1944 resulted in the capsizing of the *Tirpitz*. In late 1944, Aries, the special navigational development Lancaster PD328, wearing Pacific area roundels, made a flight around the world during which it collected data on operating Lancasters in the tropics. Barnes Wallis also developed the 22,000lb (9,979kg) Grand Slam bomb, which was intended to be carried by specially modified

Lancasters. These were first used on 14 March 1945. By VE Day, 8 May 1945, at least eleven Lancaster Is completed 100 operations.

In the final days of the war in Europe, a large-scale operation codenamed *Manna*, to drop food supplies to the starving Dutch nation, was initiated. Railway workers in occupied Holland had refused to carry out the demands of the retreating Germans and so no provisions or other necessities were being distributed around the country,

'The throbbing roar of the four engines, as they strained at the start of a take-off run, their exhaust flames lilac plumes in the twilight, really was music in the ears of operational crew. No harp or flute ever dispelled tension as they did, for it was the long waiting before take-off that was hell, not the flying to and from.'

Wing Commander Maurice Smith DFC.

For two weeks in the closing stages of the war, Lancasters of No. 115 Squadron at RAF Witchford, Cambridgeshire dropped food to the starving population of Holland in Operation *Manna*. Each aircraft was fitted with panniers capable of carrying 70 sacks of provisions. Almost 6,684 tonnes of supplies were dropped earning the Lancaster the title 'The Flying Grocer'.

with the result that a large proportion of the Dutch people were starving.

No. 115 Squadron, which had been flying Lancasters since May 1943, was the first unit to become involved in this operation when HK696 was 'lent' to Netheravon, the airfield at which parachute and glider-borne troops were taught, in late February 1945 to take part in food-dropping trials. Later, more tests were carried out at No. 115's home base at Witchford, Cambridgeshire.

Towards the end of April, operations began over the Netherlands, each Lancaster being fitted with panniers capable of

◄

*A No. 195 Squadron Lancaster drops supplies to the Dutch population as part of Operation* Manna *in April 1945, carried out to save the people from the threat of starvation.*

containing seventy sacks of provisions. Areas of the country were allocated to each squadron and markers were laid out by the Resistance to facilitate the operation. Almost the entire Dutch population came out to watch.

Another important task found for the Lancaster was that of prisoner-of-war repatriation from occupied Europe. The order for Operation *Exodus* was issued on 2 May, and just two days later the airfields at Brussels and Juvincourt were both receiving aircraft to load up with returning soldiers, sailors and airmen, twenty-four at a time. These were flown back to various reception bases all over the country, Westcott in Buckinghamshire being the main centre. Operations continued through to VE Day, by which time 74,178 PoWs had been returned home. Following the completion of Operation *Exodus* a further similar exercise, Operation *Dodge*, was mounted to bring back the personnel of the Eighth Army (the Desert Rats) from Italy. This was not completed until October–November 1945.

In the run up to D-Day (6 June 1944), Lancasters transferred their attention to targets more closely connected with the forthcoming invasion – railways, coastal guns, harbours and airfields, in addition to attacking V-weapons sites in northern France. Early in 1944, Harris had been fighting to keep his bombers over industrial targets, but he was overruled. When June arrived, the French railway system had been put out of action and could not be used to bring in German reinforcements. Bomber Command did not come under the Allied Expeditionary Air Forces Command and its aircraft did not, therefore, have the conspicuous black and white identification stripes marked around their wings and fuselage.

Targets were easily identified using $H_2S$-equipped Pathfinders, operating with a Lancaster master bomber. Raids on gun positions split open thick concrete casements, destroyed guns and put equipment out of action so, on D-Day, only one coastal battery was still in use. Signal stations had been destroyed and the enemy's communications in the landing area were 95 per cent wrecked by several small, but concentrated, Lancaster raids.

In the early hours of D-Day, Lancasters of No. 617 Squadron, led by Group Captain Leonard Cheshire VC, performed Operation *Taxable*, which they had practised beforehand. This was the difficult task of emulating two large convoys crossing the Channel at 7kt in the Pas de Calais area. Cruising at a steady 200mph (322km/h) at 3,000ft, two lines of four Lancasters spaced two miles apart with seven miles between the lines, had to fly on course for 32 seconds, then all turn through 180 degrees and backtrack for 32 seconds, before repeating the circuit, dropping Window at intervals. On partly jammed enemy radar screens, this gave an accurate simulation of shipping. Some 50 hours of practising paid off, and German coastal batteries opened up on the ghost fleet using radar prediction. A similar 'spoof invasion' was flown off Boulogne. These gave all the indications of the approach of a major Allied invasion fleet, whereas the real landings were taking place 100 miles (160km) away to the west.

On 9 June, Lancasters from No. 617 Squadron with specially bulged bomb doors used the 12,000lb (5,443kg) Tallboy penetration bomb to block the Saumur railway tunnel and hold up a German Panzer division coming from Bordeaux. This new weapon, developed by Barnes Wallis, was 38in in diameter and 21ft 6in long with four angled fins to give a slight spin.

A force of thirty-one Lancasters from Nos 9 and 617 Squadrons finally succeeded on 12 November 1944 in removing a thorn that had plagued Bomber Command since the earliest days of the war: it sank the German battleship *Tirpitz* in Alten Fjord in Norway. This was one of the war's outstanding pinpoint raids mounted from RAF Lossiemouth in Scotland. With Allied air superiority growing daily, Lancasters were able to operate with a higher degree of safety during daylight hours, and fifteen out of twenty attacks on the Ruhr between October and December 1944 were undertaken in this way.

Yet it was over Dresden that two raids evoked a bitter controversy that has still not abated. The strikes, both on the night of 13–14 April 1945, by a total of 773 Lancasters, were carried out in accordance with a plan to assist the advancing Russian forces by attacking centres of transport and munitions. The fact that the town was packed with refugees from the Eastern Front was considered superfluous in the general conduct of the war at that stage. The combination of 2,659 tons of explosives and incendiary bombs destroyed the important rail centre and seat of government, but killed somewhere between 30,000 and 50,000 people according to various estimates.

The 22,000lb (9,979kg) Grand Slam or Earthquake bomb was first used on 13 March 1945 and thirty-three Lancaster Is (all coded 'YZ') were converted to carry the weapon. The bomb, which was considered the ultimate in conventional weapons of air warfare, all but equalled the weight of the aircraft. A Lancaster from No. 617 Squadron dropped the weapon, and 35 seconds later it hit the ground only 30yd from the Bielefeld Viaduct, exploding at a depth of 100ft some 10 seconds later. The marsh erupted, throwing debris 500ft into the air, and a hundred yards of the viaduct just disappeared into the crater. Several other Grand Slams were dropped in the final stage of the war in preparation for the Rhine crossing.

'We have now achieved an accuracy with the Lancaster such that, from 20,000ft we can guarantee two direct hits on any target, 15 per cent of their bombs within 25 yards of the centre of the target, and 75 per cent of their bombs within 80 yards of it. This is precision undreamed of in the past.'

Gp Capt Leonard Cheshire VC DSO** DFC*

From the day of America's entry into the Second World War on 9 December 1941, it became Allied war strategy to defeat Germany first and then concentrate on Japan. Peace in Europe gave Bomber Command a chance to join the US Army Air Force in the Pacific to bring about the final defeat of the Japanese. The Air Staff gave priority to an RAF contribution to the air assault on Japan. The Americans asked

◄
*Lancaster VII NX780 of No 617 Squadron at RAF Waddington in mid-1945 finished in Tiger Force operations colour scheme in preparation for deploying to the Far East.*

Twenty-five new
production Lancaster
B.I(FE)s that could
house 8,000lb of bombs
internally were built by
Armstrong Whitworth
at Coventry between
October 1945 and
mid-1946. They were
originally intended for
use with the Tiger Force
in the Far East in the war
against Japan.

➤➤

The larger Avro Lincoln
was designed as
the successor to the
Lancaster, but did not
enter service until 1946.
It served with some 30
operational squadrons
until the arrival of
the first jet bombers
(Canberra and Valiant) in
the early 1950s.

if two Tallboy-equipped squadrons could be operational by 15 October 1945, as the USAAF would have no similar units ready in time. The two Lancaster squadrons, Nos 9 and 617, which had used the 12,000lb (5,443kg) bomb so successfully in the European war, were selected, their preparation started, and the necessary ships chartered for late August.

Although hostilities with Germany were over in May 1945, the conflict with Japan still raged fiercely. It had been intended

to deploy a large force of heavy bombers to the Far East, with the creation of 'Tiger Force', in the final stages of that war. It was accepted that the range/payload limitations for the Lancaster, or its successor, the Lincoln, would be severe. Admittedly, investigations into and trials of in-flight refuelling had been under way for some time, but it became clear that this offered no realistic solution in relation to the technology of the day.

Among those helping to plan Tiger Force in Washington was a former CO of No. 617 Squadron, Gp Capt Leonard Cheshire, then serving in the British Joint Staff Mission. He was well placed to understand the likely cost in human life and suffering that the forthcoming assault on Japan would entail.

A significant number of Lancaster B.I(FE)s, built by Armstrong Whitworth Aircraft, with heat-reflecting white upper surfaces but still carrying the matt black anti-search-light finish underneath, were earmarked, followed by the Lancaster IV and V (later to become the Lincoln). New Lancasters from the production lines of Vickers-Armstrong and Armstrong Whitworth were flown to Belfast for conversion to Far East standard by Short Brothers. All had the higher-powered Merlin 24 engines, with mid-upper turrets removed to compensate for a 400-gallon (1,818-litre) long-range tank fitted in the bomb-bay. American SCR-522 radios were installed in order to be compatible with equipment already in use in the South East Asia Command (SEAC) area. The bomber crew station composition was reduced to six. It was intended that the first squadron would arrive in the Pacific area on 21 November 1945. However,

Lancasters needed to re-equip the Liberator squadrons in SEAC could not be available until mid-1946 at the earliest.

Lancaster Is HK541 and SW244 were fitted by the A&AEE at Boscombe Down with a mock-up of a 1,200-gallon (5,455-litre) saddle tank built by Avro on top of the centre fuselage to increase range for Far East operations. This capacity was to supplement the 2,154 gallons (9,791 litres)

◄
*One of the Lancaster B1(FE)s prepared for Tiger Force. TW872/TL-D served with No. 35 Squadron.*

contained in the wings. But trials were not successful as the tank gave poor handling and was considered a fire hazard and vulnerable to fighter attack. The idea was dropped, but not before both modifications had undergone tropical trials in India with No. 1577 Flight.

The end of the war in Europe released many RAF squadrons for service in the Far East to help in the defeat of Japan. The Royal Australian Air Force, Royal Canadian Air Force and Royal New Zealand Air Force expressed a wish to take part in Tiger Force with their Lancaster units. However,

the majority of aircraft designed and built for service in Europe were unsuitable for operations in south-east Asia and over the Pacific, largely on account of the great distances involved. This situation had to some extent been foreseen and the Lincoln was intended for service against Japan. When it became apparent that the Lincoln was still some months from service when Nazi Germany surrendered, plans were hastily made to send a small number of Lancaster squadrons to India as part of Tiger Force. The planned fighter escort element was dropped, partly because of reports of reduced Japanese fighter activity.

The first squadron of Tiger Force was not scheduled to leave for Okinawa, via the Azores and Canada, until November 1945. With the dropping of the two atomic bombs by USAAF B-29 Superfortresses on

Hiroshima and Nagasaki on 6 and 9 August 1945 respectively, the need for Tiger Force ceased, and it was run down and disbanded on 31 October 1945. Several Lancaster squadrons were deployed to India and Burma, including No. 617 Squadron.

➤
*At the War's close, the Lancaster was retained as the standard Bomber Command aircraft. Many of them (as these No. 35 Sqn aircraft) had been modified for operation in the Far East, but the Japanese surrender prevented them from going.*

Ten Victoria Crosses, Britain's highest award for gallantry, were awarded to Lancaster aircrew. Many records of how crippled 'Lancs' defied very heavy odds and returned home safely after having sustained serious battle damage abound in the squadron records. The Lancaster VC recipients were:

**Sqn Ldr John D. Nettleton**, CO of No. 44 (Rhodesia) Squadron, for the daylight raid on Augsburg in R5508/KM-B, 17 April 1942.

**Wg Cdr Guy P. Gibson DSO\*, DFC\***, CO of No. 617 Squadron, for the Dams raid in ED932/AJ-G, 16–17 May 1943.

**Flt Lt William 'Bill' Reid** of No. 61 Squadron, for an attack on Dusseldorf, 3–4 November 1943.

**Sgt Norman C. Jackson**, Flight Engineer of No. 106 Squadron, during an attack on Schweinfurt in ME669/ZN-O, 26 April 1944.

'His [Leonard Cheshire's] VC was awarded not for any particular action but for a prolonged series of missions, in excess of 100. During his fourth tour, Wing Commander Cheshire led his squadron personally on every occasion, always undertaking the most dangerous and difficult task of making the target alone from a low level in face of strong defences. He has a reputation second to none in Bomber Command.'

Official citation to mark the achievements of determined leadership and courage over a long period, His Majesty King George VI investing Cheshire with a VC and third DSO and VC.

**Plt Off Andrew C. Mynarski**, mid-upper gunner of No. 419 Squadron (RCAF), during an attack on a target in Cambrai, France in KB726/VR-A, 12–13 June 1944 (posthumous award).

**Sqn Ldr Ian W. Bazalgette DFC** of No. 635 Squadron (PFF) as Master Bomber, for an attack on Trossy St Maxim in ND811/F2-T, 4 August 1944 (posthumous award).

**Wg Cdr Geoffrey Leonard Cheshire DSO\*\* DFC\***, CO of No. 617 Squadron, for a reputation second-to-none in Bomber Command, 8 September 1944.

**Sqn Ldr Robert A.M. Palmer DFC\***, of No. 109 Squadron (PFF), after completing 110 bombing missions in PB371/60-V, 23 December 1944 (posthumous award).

**Flt Sgt George Thompson**, of No. 9 Squadron, for an attack on the Dortmund-Ems canal in daylight in PD377/WS-U, 1 January 1945 (posthumous award).

**Capt Edwin Swales DFC**, a South African of No. 582 Squadron (PFF), as Master Bomber during an attack on Pforzheim in PB538/60-M, 23 February 1945 (posthumous award).

*FM213 is painted in the colours of Lancaster X KB726/VR-A to represent the aircraft of No. 419 Squadron RCAF in which Canadian air gunner Pilot Officer Andrew Mynarski won a Victoria Cross in June 1944.*

*Memorial to Andrew Mynarski on FM213.*

In the summer of 1945, operations were carried out under the titles Post Mortem and Spasm, these being flights over Germany to assess bomb damage and mock raids to help specialists ascertain the efficiency of German radar equipment respectively. 'Cook's Tours' over Germany gave ground crew elements a chance to see the fruits of their war efforts.

When the war ended, Lancasters continued to equip a number of Bomber Command squadrons until finally being replaced by Avro Lincolns. The last Lancaster bomber squadron (No. 49 at RAF Upwood)

converted to the Lincoln in March 1950 – this was one of the first to receive the Lancaster back in 1942, and was therefore able to boast eight years of continuous service on the type. However, the end of hostilities was followed by a rapid run-down of Bomber Command. Most of the Dominion and European squadrons disbanded or returned home.

The famous Lancaster Aries (PD328) of the Empire Central Navigation School at Shawbury completed many notable long-distance training flights between 1945 and 1948. Aries and PB873 Thor of the Empire Air Armaments School at RAF Manby became famous for round-the-world and trans-polar flights. No. 35 (Bomber) Squadron took its white-painted Lancaster B.I(FE)s, to the USA in July and August 1946 on a goodwill tour.

*Lancaster DF-N of the Central Bomber Establishment at RAF Marham in early 1946.*

'Aries 1' PD328 began its flying career in 1944 by circumnavigating the Earth in 40 days, covering a total distance of over 47,000 miles. It eventually flew nearly 200,000 miles, or the equivalent of seven more flights round the world.

No. 82 Squadron had specially modified photo reconnaissance Lancaster PRIs to complete a remarkable vast aerial survey (covering 1,216,000 sq. miles) of West, Central and East Africa between 1946 and 1952. In addition, some squadrons were based at Ein Shemer in Palestine in support of Operation *Bobcat*, to help control the flood of illegal Jewish immigrants from Europe seeking to establish their own state. Four squadrons of Lancaster B.I(FE)s and B.VII(FE)s (Nos 37, 40, 70 and 104) were based in Egypt (Shallufa and Abu Sueir) from 1945–7, patrolling the Canal Zone and carrying mail to England in bomb-bay panniers.

With so many Lancasters becoming surplus to requirements, many were used in countless trials and trial installations, including test beds for developing equipment for new postwar transport aircraft. Some of the early turbojet and turboprop engines were flown on Lancasters, not only in the usual wing position, but also in the

61

➤

*Early post-war Lancaster PB576 with freshly-painted white serial numbers under the wing and new style roundels.*

fuselage nose, bomb-bay and fuselage tail. Merlin 102s with annular radiators were tested for the Avro 688 Tudor I airliner. Lancasters were also used in gust alleviation tests, engine icing investigations, remotely-fired gun armament trials, and experiments with laminar-flow aerofoil sections.

Four Lancaster IIIs (registered G-AHJT to G-AHJW) were released to Flight Refuelling Ltd (FRL) in August 1946 and were converted at Staverton into two pairs of tanker and receiver aircraft, with bulk storage tanks and power-driven hose reels. They made a series of twenty-two transatlantic flights from May to August 1947.

These missions showed the feasibility of refuelling airliners in flight, but it was in the military field that air-to-air refuelling was to be most widely employed.

After six years of war, RAF Coastal Command emerged as a major maritime force. With the return of so many aircraft leased from the USA during the war (particularly the valuable Lockheed Hudson, B-17 Flying Fortress and B-24 Liberator), the Lancaster III underwent development to undertake the long-range maritime reconnaissance role with Coastal Command. The Short Sunderland flying boats had taken a heavy battering during the war and there was no waterborne replacement for these.

The Lancaster MR3/ GR3 became Coastal Command's main reconnaissance aircraft after Lend-Lease aircraft supplied to the RAF during the war had to be returned to the USA. Illustrated is GR3 TX269/ RL-N of No. 38 Squadron.

Testing of the Lancaster for this task had started back in November 1944 with a handful of old Mk Is, but eventually the Mk III was chosen as the Command's major variant. Two versions of the Lancaster III were quickly developed, one modified for air-sea rescue and the other for maritime reconnaissance. Some 130

Lancasters were converted by Cunliffe-Owen at Eastleigh. The mid-upper turret was removed, as was the FN.82 tail turret. Windows in the rear fuselage were installed for better observation and an enlarged astrodome was fitted at the rear of the cabin canopy. Though not able to match the performance of the US-built aircraft, they could undertake 16-hour flights with overload tanks. This gave them an operating

◀

*TW669 of the RAF St Eval Wing was one of the older Mk Is taken on by Coastal Command as a replacement for Lend-Lease Hudsons and Liberators. No. 201 Sqn was established with six ASR.IIIs in June 1946 and operated this version, modified to GR.III standard, until 1952, when they were replaced by Lockheed Neptunes.*

radius of some 1,300 miles (2,092km). Coastal Command was also responsible for meteorological and home-based photo reconnaissance work and could be called upon to contribute crews and aircraft for transportation duties.

These Lancasters were known as the GR3 or MR3, and served with nine squadrons. Some were required by No. 279 Squadron based at RAF Thornaby for air-sea rescue duties, and so were equipped with the Airborne Lifeboat Mk II. Trial dropping

➤
*The H$_2$S radar was retained in the GR3/MR3 and it also carried high-definition centimetric ASV radar.*

➤➤
*Delivered for long-range air-sea rescue, the Lancaster ASR III (RF310) seen carrying a Lindholme lifeboat.*

began in December 1945 when RF310/RL-A deployed the first all-white boat. Later, light blue boats were used, the final ones being all-yellow. Following the successful completion of trials, No. 279 Squadron's Lancaster Flight was despatched to Burma, where it became No. 1348 Flight.

The $H_2S$ radar was retained and some aircraft were fitted with high-definition centimetric ASV radar. Improved sonobuoys

and marine flares could be carried in the bomb-bay. In October 1946, with defence cuts, the Command could only muster a strength of some fifty aircraft.

In the Mediterranean area, No. 37 Squadron was based at Shallufa, Egypt and No. 38 at Luqa, Malta. They operated patrols in the Mediterranean area until

*The Shackleton was developed from the Lincoln III. It retained the Lincoln's wings and undercarriage, but introduced a shortened redesigned fuselage and Rolls-Royce Griffon engines. It entered service with Coastal Command in April 1951. Illustrated is the final AEW2 version.*

◄

*Operated by the School of Maritime Reconnaissance, Lancaster GR5 SW367 H-X was based at Blackbushe in September 1956.*

1947, when they were detached to Ein Shemer in Palestine, where they were required to carry out patrols against shipping bringing illegal Jewish immigrants to the country. This was a difficult job since most of the ships were attempting to land during the hours of darkness. Following the end of the Palestine Mandate in May 1948, the Lancasters returned to Malta. In August 1953, the first Avro Shackleton MR1s arrived, thus bringing about the end of Coastal Command's front-line Lancaster operations.

In addition, only four home-based Coastal Command squadrons flew Lancasters between 1946 and 1953, these being mainly concentrated at RAF St Eval, Cornwall. These were replaced by the Lockheed Neptune in 1953, and also eventually the Avro Shackleton. The last Lancaster GR3 sortie was flown on 15 October 1956, when RF325 left the School of Maritime Reconnaissance (SMR) at RAF St Mawgan and went direct to RAF Wroughton for scrapping.

'As the Lancaster faced its sunset with Bomber Command, with the advent of the Avro Lincoln and later the Boeing B-29 Washington, so a brief dawn appeared for the famous type in a new, and important role. It performed faithfully and amicably for Coastal as it had for Bomber Command.'

Chris Ashworth, former Coastal Command flying instructor at RAF St Eval.

Technically, the Lancaster underwent very little development and significant modifications throughout the war. Initially there was a great danger of supply problems with Merlin engines and the Hercules radial was an alternative. The Merlin supply situation was eventually saved by US Packard-built versions quickly coming on line. There were four basic versions:

**Lancaster I** – the most numerous, with 1,280hp (947kW) Rolls-Royce Merlin 20, 22 or 24 engines. It was never superseded by any other mark and continued in production until 1946.

**Lancaster I (Special)** – modified to accommodate the 8,000, 12,000 or 22,000lb bomb, but carried no $H_2S$ (the highly secret ground-mapping radar set).

**Lancaster I (FE)** – a version intended for use in the Far East with Tiger Force and the planned bombing of Japan. This force was to have consisted of twenty squadrons in two Groups.

**Lancaster II** – fitted with four 1,600hp (1,184kW) Bristol Hercules VI, and subsequently XVI, sleeve-valve radial engines. Being air-cooled, the Hercules was less vulnerable than the Merlins, with their additional glycol cooling equipment and radiators. The Rotol propellers on the radial engines rotated to the left as opposed to all Merlin-powered Lancasters which had propellers rotating in a clockwise direction.

**Lancaster III** – almost indistinguishable from the Mk I but fitted with US-built Packard Motors Merlin 28, 38 or 224 engines. Most Mk IIs featured bulged bomb-bays, originally developed to enable the 8,000lb 'Blockbuster' HC bomb to be carried.

**Did you know?**
The basic Lancaster design altered little throughout its production, a tribute to the soundness of the basic design by Roy Chadwick together with its rugged construction.

**Lancaster III (Special)** – the designation applied to 23 Lancaster IIIs modified to participate in the dams raid.

**Lancaster VI** – a little-known variant dedicated as a high-altitude bomber. Nine entered service with No. 100 Group and No. 635 Squadron in the summer of 1945 as an electronics countermeasures and radar-jamming Pathfinder Force aircraft, with improved $H_2S$ radar. It was a Mk III conversion, powered by Merlin 85 or 102s in annular cowlings, driving four-

➤

*DV178, a Lancaster I built by Metropolitan-Vickers Ltd at the Mosley Rd Works, Manchester, was converted to a MK VI powered by Rolls-Royce Merlin engines with annular cowlings and four-blade propellers.*

bladed propellers, capable of operating up to 35,000ft. It had the nose and dorsal turrets removed. It usually acted as the Master Bomber's aircraft.

**Lancaster VII** – the final production version, armed with twin 0.5in machine guns in a new Glenn Martin dorsal turret repositioned forward, and a Rose (of Gainsborough)-Rice tail turret, also mounting two 0.50in guns. This version was also destined for Tiger Force in the Pacific had the war continued. It first entered service with No. 617 Squadron at Waddington in June 1945, moving to India in January 1946

Dambusters Lancaster III ED825/G was flown by Flt Lt McCarthy on the Dams Raid and was the only aircraft of the second wave to hit the Sorpe Dam – on the tenth attempt. McCarthy was awarded the DSO for this feat. The aircraft also took part in the raid on the Antheor viaduct but was lost while undertaking an SOE mission on 10 December 1943.

Lancaster VI (a converted Mk III) JB675 seen at Boscombe Down in January 1944.

together with No. 9 Squadron, and saw action over the troublesome Indian North-West Frontier prior to partition in 1947.

**Lancaster X** – the Canadian-built version of the Mk III fitted with Packard-built Merlins.

**Lancaster ASR3** – converted by Cunliffe-Owen, with special equipment including an Airborne Lifeboat Mk IIA and Merlin 224 engines.

'The Lancaster was by far the easiest of the wartime heavy bombers to fly and, as such, any competent twin-engine pilot was able to get into it and fly it without any trouble.'

Lettice Curtis, the first woman pilot to be cleared on four-engined aircraft in February 1943, who delivered several hundred Lancasters in the following two years while serving with the Air Transport Auxiliary (ATA).

➤

*The Lancaster Mk VII was the final production version and had a Glenn Martin dorsal turret. NX612 of No. 1689 Flight is painted in Far East colour scheme.*

**Did you know?**

There are some 50,000 parts on the Lancaster, including nuts and bolts, and counting such items as engines and turrets as one. There are 96 sparking plugs in the Merlin engines.

**Lancaster GR3, subsequently redesignated MR3** – the maritime reconnaissance version.

**Lancaster PRI** – converted after the war for photographic reconnaissance duties and had their turrets removed. It served with No. 82 Squadron for aerial survey work.

There were many recorded instances of Mk Is having become Mk IIIs and vice versa, usually on major overhaul. Some were known to have flown with both British and American Merlins fitted.

A number of design projects for the Lancaster were studied by Roy Chadwick and his team as early as 1941. These included a high-altitude version with Merlin 60 engines. Another was the Stratosphere bomber with Merlin XXs but with a slave-supercharged Merlin 45 mounted internally, fitted with a blower to increase air pressure to the main engines.

With the considerable success of the Lancaster, Avro started in 1943 to examine ways of producing still better performance. This was to take advantage of lessons learned so far, together with the availability of new Rolls-Royce Merlin variants with two-speed/two-stage superchargers, which promised improved altitude performance and greater bomb loads. The changes incorporated in the Lancaster IV and V were such that a new type number and name were justified. This 'new' bomber became the Avro Type 694 Lincoln. With official reluctance to change Lancaster production over to the Lincoln in late 1944 to early 1945, the new aircraft missed the closing stages of the Second World War. The ultimate development of the lineage, which began with the Manchester in 1939, was the Shackleton maritime patrol aircraft which was developed from the Lincoln and was first flown in 1949.

The Avro 685 York was a four-engined transport developed in a period of six months in 1942. Avro combined the Lancaster's wings, tail unit (with a third central fin), engines and undercarriage with a new, more capacious, slab-sided fuselage. It was conceived to exploit more fully the long-distance load-carrying capability of the Lancaster. The wings were shoulder-

**Did you know?**

In June 1941, Rolls-Royce proposed a five-engined Lancaster. Basically, it featured a single-speed Merlin (45 or 46 series) installed within the fuselage driving a huge slave supercharger that supplied air, via ducting, to the blowers of the four wing-mounted engines, providing in effect, two-stage supercharging.

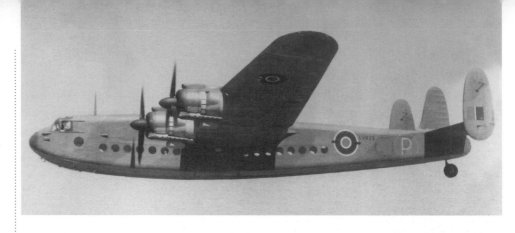

**Did you know?**

Among projected Avro versions was a high-speed Lancaster mailplane and a York GR flying boat, utilising a Lancaster wing.

mounted rather than in the mid-position as on the Lancaster. First flown on 5 July 1942, only a small number of Yorks were constructed during the war. They had been produced 'semi-officially' as an agreement with the US government – neither material nor labour was to be used in Britain for transport aircraft as they would be supplied as Lend-Lease equipment, thus leaving British industry to concentrate on military aircraft. This worked very well, and reverse Lend-Lease gave the Americans several British military aircraft. Eventually, 257 Yorks were built for the RAF and British Overseas Airways Corporation (BOAC), while other civilian users postwar flew mainly ex-RAF aircraft. All but one of the Yorks were Rolls-Royce Merlin-powered Mk Is, the sole experimental Mk II being powered by Bristol Hercules radials. The

RAF used the York, of which forty examples did sterling service during the Berlin Airlift until 1957, and the last civilian examples were withdrawn in the early 1960s.

In addition to the York, Avro decided to produce a Lancaster transport as the Type 691 Lancastrian. The winding down of Lancaster production in 1945 allowed airframes on the production line to be completed as Lancastrians. A total of eighty-two were built at Woodford, with the first (PD180, later VB873/G-AGLF) being flown on 17 January 1945. These aircraft played a vital part in the proving of postwar civil air routes.

The first airline to use the Lancastrian was Trans-Canada Air Lines which initiated the design with a requirement for a passenger-carrying transatlantic aircraft. Six examples were purchased for its fleet.

The basic Lancastrians were externally similar to the bomber, with military equipment removed and lengthened fairings covering the nose and tail sections. Internally a rudimentary 'luxurious' cabin was fitted, with seating initially for nine passengers, although this was later increased to thirteen. The very basic

'The York was built with the purpose of bridging the gap between wartime military transport and postwar commercial airlines and as such it was the best of the military conversion batch that included the Lancaster, Whitley, Halton (Halifax conversion), Stirling and Warwick. It is difficult to believe that a finer aeroplane could be found for conversion than the Lancaster, and yet the Lancastrian, which was a less radical conversion than the York, lost some of the flight characteristics of its parent aircraft.'

Capt Eric 'Winkle' Brown RN, Test Pilot.

passenger transport was cramped and unpressurised. Launched as an interim 'airliner', it remained in service much longer than planned, mainly due to the failure of Avro's first purpose-built postwar airliner, the Tudor.

BOAC received the first batch of twenty-three Lancastrian Is during 1945 for the route to Australia. Although they were relatively fast and had good range, they were hardly an economic proposition. Most had been scrapped by the early 1950s. The Lancastrian C2 was the RAF's equivalent of the civil Mk I. Thirty-three examples were delivered, the first being received in October 1945. RAF Lancastrians were used for general purpose transport duties, conversion training and by the Empire Flying School and Empire Navigation School.

The final Lancastrian variant was the C4, only eight of which were delivered to the RAF. They saw very limited RAF service and were soon disposed of on the civil market. Like the York, civil Lancastrians saw extensive use on the Berlin Airlift between 1948 and 1949.

**Did you know?**
The first civil conversion of the Lancaster was done on the British-built R5727 in August 1942 by Victory Aircraft Ltd for Trans Canada Air Lines. Extra fuel tankage and seats for 10 passengers were installed, and the Lancaster was registered CF-CMS. It inaugurated the Dorval-Prestwick transatlantic service on 22 July 1943.

*Lancaster VI ND784, known as the 'Lancaster Universal Test Bed', seen here at RAE in April 1943. It had four Merlin XXs and a 2,600lb st Armstrong Siddeley ASX in the bomb-bay. It later had four 1,750hp Merlin 85s in annular cowlings and an Armstrong Siddeley Mamba in the nose.*

Between 1943 and 1956, twelve Lancasters in the UK (together with two Lancaster Xs in Canada) and nine Lancastrians were used as test beds for new British, and occasionally foreign, turboprop and jet engines under development. They also saw similar use in relation to later marks of well-known piston engines such as the Merlin 102, 600, 620 and 621, and the Griffon 57. Jet engines were usually mounted in outboard nacelles, replacing the outer Merlins.

The first jet test bed was Lancaster prototype BT308 which, in 1943, was fitted with a Metrovick F.2 in the extreme tail. The F.2/1 and F.2/4 Beryl jets were also flown in the tail of Lancaster II LL735/G. Sometimes, two different engines were flown in one aircraft at the same time, as on Lancaster III SW342 which had an Armstrong Siddeley Mamba in the nose with a de-icing rig and an afterburning Adder pure jet by the same manufacturer in the tail.

A Swedish STAL Stovern turbojet was test-flown in an outsize nacelle under the fuselage of Lancaster 80001 of the Royal Swedish Air Force. It was subsequently flown with an RB2B Ghost in the nacelle with reheat, this engine built under a de Havilland licence by Svenska Flygmotor AB for the Saab J29 programme.

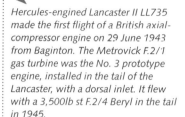

Hercules-engined Lancaster II LL735 made the first flight of a British axial-compressor engine on 29 June 1943 from Baginton. The Metrovick F.2/1 gas turbine was the No. 3 prototype engine, installed in the tail of the Lancaster, with a dorsal inlet. It flew with a 3,500lb st F.2/4 Beryl in the tail in 1945.

Left: Lancaster III SW342 was modified in 1949 to take a nose-mounted Armstrong Siddeley Mamba propeller-turbine. It was delivered to Billeswell for icing tests and later was fitted with an Adder turbojet and then a Viper in the tail.

Right: Lancaster 80001 (ex-RAF RA805) of the Swedish Air Force at Malmslatt was used to test the Stal Dovern axial flow and later the DH Ghost jet engines before it crashed on 8 May 1956.

➤

*Lancaster X FM209 was converted to take two Orenda axial jets in the outboard positions. The 6,000lb thrust Orenda was Avro Canada's second incursion into the gas turbine field. It was first flown in July 1950.*

➤

*The RCAF used Lancaster 10DC KB851 in the 1950s to test Ryan Firebee drones, seen here carried under the outer wings.*

The ex-bomber made a significant contribution to the development of new aero engines in the postwar era. All the major British engine manufacturers used Lancasters as test beds for the development of their jet engines. Rolls-Royce was the exception, as it employed Lancastrians and the Lincoln. However, it did use Lancaster III NG465 to test its Dart turboprop fitted to its nose. First flown on 10 October 1947, it also had a circular icing rig mounted in front of its spinner for water droplet artificial icing tests, in conjunction with two 100-gallon water tanks in the rear fuselage.

Vickers-Armstrong used PP791 fitted with Merlin 600s for braking propeller development, and Armstrong Whitworth operated TW911 for Python I turboprop development, fitted outboard.

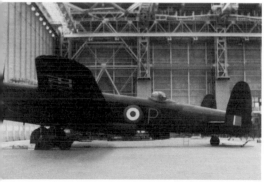

In Canada, Lancaster X FM205 was used as a test bed for Avro Chinook TR Mk II engines, mounted in outer nacelles. FM209 subsequently had two Avro Orenda jet engines in its outer nacelles. A Lancaster Mk X was converted to carry Ryan Firebee drones.

The Lancaster and its close relatives also played a major part in the refinement of air-to-air refuelling, being operated by FRL at Tarrant Rushton in Dorset. Experiments in the practice had been conducted by FRL and the Bombing Development Unit in the summer of 1944, using Lancasters ND648 and NE147, including the critical night rendezvous, entailing tanker and receiver aircraft flying sufficiently close to link hoses without the danger of collision. Lancaster Is PP755 and RE131 were also used for testing various parts of the Bristol 167 Brabazon 1 airliner's flight control system.

*Avro Lancastrian Mk10-PP registered G-AKDO in September 1947, was former Lancaster KB729 and served with Flight Refuelling Ltd at Tarrant Rushton, Dorset, until May 1951.*

*RE131, one of two Lancaster Is used as a Bristol Brabazon flying controls test aircraft based at Filton.*

War surplus Lancasters found a ready market among foreign powers and A.V. Roe overhauled fifteen surplus Mk Is built by Metro-Vick which were flown in 1948–9 to Buenos Aires to equip Air Regiment No. 1 (Bomber), Argentine Air Force. There they replaced the Martin 139WAA. Three were later converted to transports. The last of the type was finally retired in 1968 after twenty years of service.

Royal Canadian Air Force squadrons had operated alongside the RAF from airfields in England during the Second World War. Postwar, the RCAF had 228 Lancaster Xs on strength, comprising some aircraft which had not crossed the Atlantic to join the RAF, and about 200 survivors of the war which returned to their country of origin after hostilities had ended. Many suffixes were used to identify the different tasks performed by the aircraft. With its very strong airframe, some were converted as water bombers for fire control in Canadian forest areas. The aerial reconnaissance versions were fitted with AN/APS-42B search radar and no fewer than ten cameras.

▼
*Lancaster X NG347 was flown by the RCAF from Canadian bases in North Yorkshire.*

WU-13 was one of 22 Mk VIIs delivered to the French Aéronavale. It was modified to full ASR standard at 38 MU at Llandow, South Wales, and was still in service in New Caledonia in the early 1960s.

The RCAF retired its last Lancaster in April 1964.

Ordered in 1948, nine Mk Is, refurbished at Bracebridge Heath, were delivered to the Royal Egyptian Air Force in June 1950, but were little used due to shortage of spares, bombs and ammunition and they sat out in the sun at Almaza. The delay in delivery was due to the Arab-Israeli war of 1948.

They were still in existence during the Suez campaign of 1956 and were destroyed by RN strike aircraft.

In March 1952, thirty-two Lancaster Is and twenty-two VIIs were also reconditioned to RAF maritime reconnaissance standard at Woodford and Langar for the French Aéronavale under the Western Union defence plans. Long-range tanks were

fitted, dorsal turrets removed and ventral ASV radar installed. Life-raft attachment points were also added. They went into French overseas service for maritime reconnaissance from bases in North Africa. Some were operational with Escadrille 9S at Noumea, New Caledonia, in the South Pacific.

A further five 'civil' Lancaster VIIs were delivered in early 1954 to the French Coast Guard for special duties, based at Maison Blanche in Algeria and Agadir, Morocco, but flown by French Navy crews. All were retired by May 1965, being replaced by the Lockheed P2V Neptune.

The Soviet Air Force assembled two examples from those that had force-landed in Russia during the first *Tirpitz* raids. Two Lancasters found their way into the inventory of the Royal Australian Air Force.

Lancaster B.VII NX611 (built by Austin Motors, Birmingham) was operated by the French Aéronavale as WU-15 in New Caledonia until early 1963. It was purchased by the Historic Aircraft Preservation Society and flown to Sydney, Australia on 13 August 1964. It was delivered to Biggin Hill on 13 May 1965 during the Air Fair.

NX611/G-ASXX at Biggin Hill in May 1965

➤
*From 1954 to 1962
Lancaster PA474 was
based at Cranfield,
Bedfordshire, with the
College of Aeronautics.*

The Royal Air Force's Battle of Britain Memorial Flight (BBMF) maintains Lancaster PA474 *City of Lincoln* in airworthy condition at RAF Coningsby, and it continues to take part in flying displays and flypasts. Built by Vickers-Armstrong at Hawarden, North Wales, as a basic Lancaster I reconnaissance/bomber, it was modified to Far East standards for use with Tiger Force in 1944–5. Due to the sudden ending of the war in Asia, the aircraft was re-modified as a PR.I by Armstrong Whitworth for use on photo

reconnaissance work by 'B' Flight of No. 82 Squadron at RAF Benson. For this purpose, two American K-17 cameras were fitted in the $H_2S$ scanner position beneath the fuselage. All the turrets were removed and PA474 was then engaged for four years on a photographic survey of the African continent, carrying the identification code letter 'M' and operating out of Takoradi in Ghana. Some missions lasted for up to 14 hours and internal supplementary fuel tanks were fitted.

On PA474's return to the UK it was loaned, from 26 May 1952, to FRL at Tarrant Rushton, Dorset, to be used as a pilotless drone, but then the Air Ministry decided to use a Lincoln instead. From there, the aircraft moved to the RAE at Cranfield in March 1954, where it was employed as a flying test bed for equipment used in laminar flow swept wing flight trials. The Handley Page trial wing was mounted vertically on the upper rear fuselage for test purposes.

In October 1963, the Lancaster was adopted by the Ministry of Defence Air Historical Branch (AHB) for future display in the proposed RAF Museum at Hendon, and was stored in the open at RAF Henlow. It was subsequently flown to RAF Wroughton where it was painted in a camouflage scheme, though without squadron markings. During this time it took part in film work. Later in 1964, it was moved to Henlow in preparation for display at Hendon. Then it was decided to keep PA474 flying, so the bomber was flown from Henlow to RAF Waddington, on 18 August 1965, at the request of the CO of No. 44 Squadron who fortunately was

▲
PA474 was fitted with a small section of swept wing on its fuselage for laminar flow trial at Cranfield.

an enthusiastic aviation historian. It was considered more appropriate to allocate the aircraft to an operational station where sufficient skilled technicians were available to maintain it in flying trim, and return it to full airworthy condition.

At Waddington, a restoration programme began after the airframe was found to be structurally sound. It was still minus its nose and mid-upper gun turrets, which took several years to complete. Unlike

➤

*After restoration at Waddington for the RAF Museum, PA474 was flown again on 7 November 1967. It did not have a mid-upper turret fitted at this time.*

**Did you know?**

During the 1977–8 major overhaul of PA474, some 100,000 corroded magnesium rivets were replaced and new fuel tanks were installed in the wings.

➤

*Lancaster PA474 flying with the BBMF's Spitfire and Hurricane in 1990.*

its wartime night bomber counterparts, PA474 was not fitted with flame-damping exhaust shrouds. The aircraft eventually joined the Battle of Britain Flight at RAF Coltishall in November 1973, joining the Spitfires and Hurricanes of the Historic Aircraft Flight. It was at this point that the unit was renamed as the Battle of Britain Memorial Flight. A mid-upper turret was discovered in Argentina and brought back by the Royal Navy aboard HMS *Hampshire* before being fitted to PA474 in 1975. That same year, the aircraft was adopted by the City of Lincoln.

In March 1976, the whole flight moved north to RAF Coningsby, where it continues to be based. To prolong the airframe life, the aircraft is kept as light as possible for display purposes. Maximum speed is limited to 200mph (322km/h), though

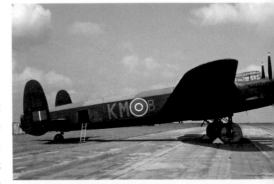

in practice it is not flown above 170mph (275km/h), at which it burns around 200 gallons of fuel per hour. A typical fuel load is 650–950 imperial gallons, which gives the Lancaster sufficient endurance to complete a round-robin flight taking in three display appearances without refuelling. It is flown very carefully, restricted to a maximum of 1.5g in manoeuvres and a maximum take-off weight of 47,000lb (21,319kg), compared to 65,000lb (29,4894kg) or more in wartime operational use.

Every six years, the Lancaster undergoes major servicing and at this time receives a change of colour scheme and markings. Initially, until 1979, it was given the code KM-B of a famous Lancaster of No. 44 Squadron in which Sqn Ldr J.D. Nettleton VC took part in the historic low-level daylight attack on the U-boat engine

In the 1970s PA474 carried the code letters KM-B of No. 44 Squadron to represent the 1942 Augsburg raid aircraft flown by Sqn Ldr Nettleton VC.

In the 1980s PA474 was first painted with the code letters SR-D of No. 101 Squadron.

> PA474's colour scheme changed in the 1990s. It now represented W4964 with code WS-J and Johnnie Walker Still Going Strong nose art. This was an aircraft that took part in the Tirpitz raid in November 1944.

factory at Augsburg in April 1942. It was then given the AJ-G code of No. 617 Squadron's ED932, the personal Lancaster of Wg Cdr Guy Gibson VC DSO* DFC*, which he flew during the dams raid. This was followed by a period as SR-D to represent an aircraft of No. 101 Squadron, and then the PM-M$^2$ code of ED888 while with No. 103 Squadron.

In 1994, another change occurred, this time to depict W4964 with Johnnie Walker *Still Going Strong* markings on its nose (W4964 was unofficially adopted by the famous Scotch Whisky firm) as carried in 1944. The lines of bombs – yellow bombs for night operations, white bombs denoting day operations and an oversize bomb representing the 12,000lb (5,443kg) bomb dropped on the *Tirpitz* on 12 November 1944 – were faithfully

◄
*Left: Close-up of the 'Still Going Strong' artwork on the nose of BBMF Lancaster PA474.*

*Right: In 2000 PA474's markings changed to QR-M as on EE176 Mickey the Moucher of No. 61 Squadron, an aircraft that flew more than 100 wartime operational missions.*

'I could see visions of the past through the windscreen. I would have known it was a Lancaster when I climbed in, even if I had been blindfolded. Every aircraft has its own smell.'

Air Vice-Marshal H.B. Martin, AOC No. 38 Group, a No. 617 Squadron pilot on the dams raid, on climbing into PA474 after a lapse of twenty-four years.

◄
*PA474 in its current (2008) paint scheme.*

 *From 2007 PA474's port side represented No. 550 Squadron's HW-R Phantom of the Ruhr.*

 *. . . and on the starboard side it was marked as BQ-B of No. 100 Squadron.*

➤➤ *Top left: The Phantom of the Ruhr artwork was revealed for the first time in May 2007.*

*Top right: PA474 on major overhaul at Coventry in December 2006.*

*Bottom: The Lancaster's cockpit when it was on major overhaul with Air Atlantique.*

reproduced. This Lancaster had been a veteran of 106 operations. From 2000, PA474 was painted in the markings originally worn by Lancaster III EE176/QR-M *Mickey the Moocher* of No. 61 Squadron, No. 5 Group, based at RAF Skellingthorpe in Lincolnshire. EE176 was one of only thirty-five Lancaster centurions – aircraft that flew and survived in excess of 100 missions.

During the winter of 2006–7, it was decided that PA474 would carry the unit markings that were assigned to a veteran of 100 Second World War missions, Lancaster EE139, initially of No. 100 Squadron and latterly of No. 550 Squadron. Named *Phantom of the Ruhr* with the code letters HW-R of No. 100 Squadron and thirty mission markings on the left-hand side, it has the codes BQ-B of No. 550 Squadron

on the right. It was originally decided that PA474 would be in No. 100 Squadron colours, but the Officer Commanding the BBMF, Sqn Ldr Al Pinner, received such a volume of mail from No. 550 Squadron members, with whom she flew a further ninety-one missions, that it was decided to commemorate both squadrons. The new markings were applied following a major overhaul of the airframe by Air Atlantique.

The world's population of airworthy Lancasters doubled on 11 September 1988, when Mk X FM213 (painted as KB726) took to the air again at Hamilton, Ontario in Canada. A Canadian-built example, it was built in July 1945 and was delivered to the RCAF for the maritime reconnaissance role. It was struck off charge on 30 June 1964 and was purchased by the Royal Canadian Legion at Goedrich, Ontario. The bomber was mounted on poles and painted in the colours of Lancaster X KB726/VR-A

of No. 419 Squadron, RCAF. This was the aircraft in which Plt Off Andrew Mynarski, a Canadian air gunner, gained his Victoria Cross on the night of 12–13 June 1944. He suffered severe burns trying to save his rear gunner, who was trapped in his burning turret. This is the scheme that the aircraft flies in today as a 'living' memorial to him.

In the 1980s, the Canadian Warplane Heritage (CWH) group purchased the airframe for restoration to flying condition. Placed on the Canadian civil register as C-GVRA, it is the world's only civilian-operated airworthy Lancaster. During the summer of 1988, FM213 was repainted again as Lancaster X KB726/VR-A.

➤ *The famous Lancaster I R5868/PO-S 'S for Sugar', veteran of 137 missions, was a gate guardian at RAF Scampton from 1958 before going to the RAF Museum on 24 August 1970.*

**Did you know?**

A total of thirty-four Lancasters each flew a hundred or more operational missions during the Second World War.

➤➤ *Lancaster I R5868 in the RAF Museum's Bomber Command Hall at Hendon. Its scoreboard of missions is shown under the cockpit.*

The following essentially complete Lancaster airframes are preserved and on display. Most survivors owe their existence to postwar service in either France or Canada. The only two airworthy aircraft are 'KB726' in Canada and PA474 in the UK.

**Mk I R5868** Bomber Command Hall, RAF Museum Hendon, Greater London. Completed 137 missions with Nos 83 and 467 Squadrons. Bears the inscription No Enemy Plane will fly over the Reich Territory and coded PO-S.

**Mk I W4783** ANZAC Hall, Australian War Memorial, Canberra, Australia. Completed eighty-nine missions as AR-G with No. 460 Squadron.

**Mk X FM104** Toronto Aerospace Museum, Downsview, Ontario, Canada. Ex-No. 428 Squadron. Converted to a Mk 10(MR)

as CX104 and flew with the RCAF until 1964.

**Mk X FM136** Aerospace Museum, Calgary, Alberta, Canada. Postwar, served as a Mk 10(MR), RX136.

**Mk X FM159** Nanton Lancaster Society and Air Museum, Nanton, Alberta, Canada. Postwar, served as a Mk 10(MR), RX159, with No. 407 Squadron, RCAF.

Time has not marred my grim old frame,
To your fading eyes I am the same,
Look well, all strangers standing there,
For I'm the mighty LANCASTER.

From 'Showpiece . . . Lancaster' by Walter Scott
(No. 630 Squadron).

**Mk X FM212** Jackson Park Sunken Gardens, Windsor, Ontario, Canada. Post-war, served as a Mk 10(MR), MN212, with No. 408 Squadron, RCAF.

**Mk X 'KB726'** Canadian Warplane Heritage Museum, Hamilton, Ontario, Canada. Delivered to the RCAF as FM213 in August 1946. Operated as Mk 10(MR) until retired in June 1964. Acquired by CWH in 1977 and rebuilt at Hamilton from November 1979. Registered C-GVRA and painted as KB726, it was first flown on 11 September 1988.

**Mk X KB839** Greenwood, Nova Scotia, Canada. Did see action during the Second World War with Nos 431 and 419 Squadrons. Converted to a Mk 10(MR) postwar for service with the RCAF.

**Mk X KB882** St Jacques Airport, Edmundston, New Brunswick, Canada. A wartime

**Did you know?**
In order that this famous type should not be forgotten, Lancaster I R5868, veteran of 137 wartime sorties with Nos 83 and 467 Squadrons, was selected for preservation. Originally mounted at the main gate of RAF Scampton, its former base, it is now in the Bomber Command Hall of the RAF Museum at Hendon.

aircraft as NA-R with No. 428 Squadron. Served as a Mk 10(MR), MN882, with RCAF postwar.

**Mk X KB889** Imperial War Museum, Duxford, Cambridgeshire. Preserved in its wartime colours as NA-I of No. 428 Squadron. Appeared on the British Civil Register as G-LANC in the 1980s on return from Canada and acquired by the Imperial War Museum.

**Mk X KB944** Canada Aviation Museum, Ottawa, Ontario, Canada. Served on No. 425 Squadron as KW-K during the Second World War and became a standard

Lancaster X with the RCAF until February 1957.

**Mk X KB976** Fantasy of Flight Museum, Polk City, Florida, USA (in storage). Formerly LQ-K with No. 405 Squadron but did not see action. Later became a Mk 10(AR), MN976, with No. 408 Squadron, RCAF.

Entered Canadian civil register as a water bomber (CF-TQC) in 1964.

**Mk VII NX611** Lincolnshire Aviation Heritage Centre, East Kirkby, Lincolnshire (taxiable). Did not see service until delivered to the French Navy as WU-15 in 1952. Now wears the markings of Nos 57 and 630

*Now on display in the Museum of Transport and Technology, Auckland, Lancaster NX665 is painted in Second World War RAF Bomber Command markings.*

Squadrons which were based at East Kirkby during the Second World War. Named *Just Jane*.

**Mk VII NX622** RAAF Association Aviation Heritage Museum, Bull Creek, Perth,

Australia. Did not see service with the RAF but went to the French Navy as WU-16 from 1952–62. Preserved in Bomber Command colour scheme as LL847 of No. 463 Squadron, coded JO-D.

**Mk VII NX665** Museum of Transport and Technology (MOTAT), Austin, Auckland, New Zealand. Formerly WU-13 of French Navy. Gifted to New Zealand and is painted as PB457 of No. 101 Squadron, coded SR-V on the port side, and as ND752 of No. 75 (RNZAF) Squadron, coded AA-O on the starboard side.

**Mk I PA474** Battle of Britain Memorial Flight, RAF Coningsby, Lincolnshire. (See PA474 Flies On.)

**Mk VII NX664** Musée de l'Air, Le Bourget, Paris, France. Former French Navy WU-21, still under restoration.

**Engines:**

Prototype: Four 1,145hp (847kW) Rolls-Royce Merlin X

Mk I: Four 1,280hp/1,620hp (947/1,198kW) Rolls-Royce Merlin XX, 22 or 24

Mk II: Four 1,650hp (1,221kW) Bristol Hercules VI or XVI

Mk III: Four 1,300hp (962kW) Packard Merlin 28; 1,390hp (1,028kW) Merlin 38; or 1,640hp (1,214kW) Merlin 224

Mk VI: Four 1,750hp (1,295kW) Rolls-Royce Merlin 85 or 102

Mk VII: Four 1,620hp (1,198kW) Rolls-Royce Merlin 24

Mk X: Four 1,300hp (962kW) Packard Merlin 28; 1,390hp (1,028kW) Merlin 38; or 1,640hp (1,214kW) Merlin 224

**Max speed:**

Mks I, III and X 287mph (469km/h)

Mk II 270mph (435km/h)

Mk VII 275mph (442km/h)

**Cruising speed:**

160–170mph (257–273km/h) to a target; 200mph (321km/h) after bomb release

**Wingspan:** 102ft 0in (31.08m)

**Length:** 69ft 6in (21.18m)

**Height:** 20ft 6in (6.18m)

**Armament:**

Machine guns: Two 0.303in (nose and

**Did you know?**

The Lancaster began life in 1941 with an all-up weight of 55,000lb and ended the war weighing in at 72,000lb, an increase of over 30 per cent.

Max all-up weight: 68,000lb (30,849kg)
Range: 2,530 miles (4,072km)
Service Ceiling: 24,500ft (7,468m)
Number built: 7,377
Entered service: December 1941

Lancaster I: 3,432 (including 3 prototypes)
Lancaster II: 300 (Armstrong Whitworth, Coventry)
Lancaster III: 3,035 (including 23 aircraft specially modified to carry the Barnes Wallis dam-buster bomb)
Lancaster VII: 180 (Austin Motors, Longbridge, Birmingham)
Lancaster X: 430 (Victory Aircraft Ltd, Malton, Ontario, Canada)
Eight Lancaster VIs were converted from Mk IIIs

Total new production: 7,377

*Lancaster BX KB889 is preserved at the Imperial War Museum, Duxford, Cambridgeshire.*

dorsal turret) four 0.303in (rear turret)
Bomb load (normal): 14,000lb (6,350kg) various sizes/combinations
Special load: Single 12,000lb (5,443kg), or 22,000lb (9,979kg) bombs
Mine-laying: Six 1,000lb (454kg) sea mines

The main manufacturer was A.V. Roe & Co. Ltd at Chadderton (Manchester) and Woodford, which also operated vast new shadow factories at Yeadon (today Leeds/Bradford Airport) and Langar, Nottinghamshire. Sub-contract was also by Armstrong Whitworth Aircraft at Coventry and Bitteswell; Austin Motors Ltd at Longbridge, Birmingham; Metropolitan-Vickers at Trafford Park, Manchester (transported to Woodford for final assembly), and Vickers-Armstrong Ltd at Castle Bromwich and Hawarden (Chester). An order for 200 from Short and Harland at Belfast was not proceeded with. Component manufacturers were located throughout the UK. The total was further swelled by Victory Aircraft Ltd of Toronto, a company formed by the National Steel Corporation of Canada especially for that purpose, under government control. (Postwar the company was purchased by Hawker Siddeley and became known as Avro Canada.) Other factories, such as the LMS Railway Works at Derby, became Lancaster repair and maintenance depots.

Spares produced for Avro Repair Units

*Lancaster B.VII NX611 Just Jane is at the Lincolnshire Aviation Centre, East Kirkby.*

to replace either battle-damaged or crash-damaged parts would have yielded another 622 airframes. These spares were used by the extensive Lancaster repair organisation to rebuild 3,816 aircraft. In 1943, 55 per cent of all aircraft supplied to the RAF were from the repair organisations.

**1940** **20 February**: Avro Manchester development powered by four Rolls-Royce Merlin engines discussed with the Air Ministry.

**1940** **September**: Air Ministry accepted that Lancaster production should go ahead.

**1941** **9 January**: First flight from Ringway of prototype (BT308), originally known as the Manchester III, with four Merlin engines instead of two Vultures.

**1941** **27 January**: Prototype Lancaster BT308 flew to Boscombe Down for preliminary acceptance trials.

**1941** **13 May**: Second prototype (DG595) made its maiden flight. This aircraft was more representative of production Mk Is with Merlin 20s, the definitive tailplane/fin arrangement and armament.

**1941** **September**: Prototype BT308 delivered to No. 44 Squadron at RAF Waddington for Service trials.

**1941** **31 October**: First production Lancaster I (L7527) flown.

**1941** **22 November**: Fourth production Lancaster, the first to be earmarked for Service use, was flown.

**1941** **26 November**: Maiden flight of Lancaster II DT810 with Bristol Hercules VI sleeve-valve radial engines.

**1941** **24 December**: No. 44 (Rhodesia) Squadron received its first Lancasters to replace Handley Page Hampdens.

**1942** **14 January**: The second front-line unit to receive the Lancaster was

No. 97 Squadron at RAF Coningsby (moving to Woodhall Spa on 2 March).

1942 **3–4 March**: First Lancaster operation – a mine-laying sortie in the Heligoland Bight off the north coast of Germany by No. 97 Squadron.

1942 **4 March**: The first Lancaster to be lost (R5493 of No. 44 Squadron), which failed to return from a mine-laying mission near Lorient.

1942 **10–11 March**: The first night bombing raid against a land target in Germany was flown by Lancasters of No. 44 Squadron against targets at Essen.

1942 **16 April**: No. 83 Squadron at RAF Coningsby received Lancasters.

1942 **17 April**: A dozen Lancasters from

Nos 44 and 97 Squadrons carried out the daring low-level raid on the MAN Diesel factory at Augsburg.

1942 **30 May**: The first 'thousand-bomber raid' on Cologne. Sixty-eight Lancasters took part; only one was lost.

1942 **August**: The first installation of a Packard Merlin in a Lancaster (R5849), the aircraft used by Rolls-Royce for tests.

1942 **August**: A 'pattern' Lancaster I (R5727) was sent to Canada for Victory Aircraft.

1942 **18–19 August**: Lancasters of No. 83 Squadron took part in the first operation by the Pathfinder Force (subsequently to become No. 8 Group in Bomber Command) during a raid on Flensburg.

**1942**  **October**: Armstrong Whitworth delivered its first Lancaster II (DS601).

**1942**  **17 October**: Ninety-four Lancasters attacked the Schneider factory at Le Creusot in eastern France near the Swiss border, another daring daylight raid.

**1943**  **11–12 January**: First operational mission by a Lancaster II. Some 60 per cent of Lancaster IIs were lost on operations, many due to their inability to climb to a reasonable height. Maximum height with a full load was only 15,000ft.

**1943**  **28 February**: Air Staff gave the 'go-ahead' for full-scale trials prior to the Dams raid.

**1943**  **5 March**: Battle of the Ruhr opened with Lancasters using the newly introduced bombing and navigation aid 'Oboe'.

**1943**  **18 April**: The first production-modified Lancaster (ED864/G) arrived at RAF Scampton for No. 617 Squadron, the twentieth being delivered on 13 May.

**1943**  **16–17 May**: Operation *Chastise* – the Dams Raid.

**1943**  **24 July**: Operation *Gomorrah*, the firestorm attack on Hamburg and the first use of 'Window'. 791 bombers took part, of which 354 were Lancasters.

**1943**  **25 July**: The first Lancaster transport conversion, from Mk I R5727, provided to Victory Aircraft as a pattern aircraft prior to Canadian production, inaugurated a transatlantic service, operated by

▲

*Lancasters without a dorsal turret had bomb bay modifications for the Dams Raid, but British security did not release details until 1963. Shown here is ED817 AJ-C of No 617 Squadron that was operated out of RAF Scampton.*

Trans-Canadian Air Lines as CF-CMS.

**1943 August**: First major raid on the German experimental rocket base at Peenemunde on the Baltic Coast.

**1943 6 August**: The first Canadian-built Lancaster X (KB700) made its maiden flight.

**1943 16–17 August**: The last Lancaster raid on Turin before the Italian surrender.

**1943 15–16 September**: The first 12,000lb light-case bomb was dropped by a Lancaster on the Dortmund-Ems canal at Ladbergen.

**1943 17 September**: First Lancaster built in Canada flew the Atlantic to the UK in 9 hours 30 minutes.

**1943 7–8 October**: No. 101 Squadron Lancasters used the 'Airborne Cigar' communications system operationally for the first time.

**1943 3–4 November**: The radar device known as Gee-H was used by Lancaster Pathfinders for the first time in an attack on Dusseldorf.

**1943**  **10 November**: $H_2S$ Mk III Lancasters delivered to Nos 83 and 97 (PFF) Squadrons.

**1943**  **18–19 November**: The Battle of Berlin opened with a raid by 440 Lancasters.

**1944**  **January**: Lancaster III JB675 was first flown with Merlin 85s.

**1944**  **20 January**: The first British-built Lancaster to be civilianised, DV379/G-AGJI, camouflaged and with neat fairings in place of nose and tail turrets, was handed over to BOAC's newly created Development Flight at Hurn.

**1944**  **8 June**: The first aircraft to carry the 12,000lb Tallboy deep penetration bomb which blocked the Saumur railway tunnel.

**1944**  **9 June**: First flight of the Lancaster IV, redesignated Lincoln in August.

**1944**  **16–17 June**: The first attack on V1 sites in the Pas de Calais area by 236 Lancasters.

**1944**  **October**: Planning for Tiger Force began.

**1944**  **21 October:** Lancaster PD328 *Aries* embarked on the first round-the-world flight from the UK. The aircraft took off from Shawbury and returned 53 days later, on 14 December, having flown a total of almost 36,000nm and 202 flying hours.

**1944**  **12 November**: Eighteen Lancasters from No. 617 Squadron and thirteen from No. 9 Squadron, using 12,000lb Tallboy bombs,

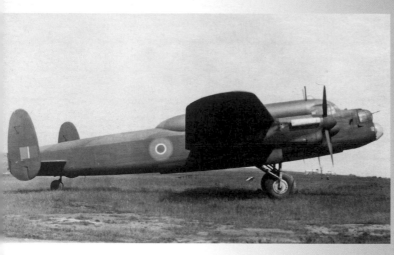

▲
*One of two long-range Lancasters specially modified with 1,200gal saddle tanks for possible use by the Tiger Force.*

bombers, including 748 Lancasters, attacked Dortmund.

**1945** **19 March**: The first Lancaster I (Special) dropped the mammoth 22,000lb (10,000kg) Grand Slam bomb on the Arnsberg Bridge in Germany.

**1945** **1 April**: Operation Manna food-dropping missions by No. 115 Squadron. 3,156 Lancaster sorties were flown to the Low Countries.

**1945** **24 April**: One of the most satisfactory raids of the war for 361 Lancaster crews was the daylight attack on Hitler's 'Eagle's Nest' retreat at Berchtesgaden in the Bavarian Alps.

**1945** **25–6 April**: The last Lancaster raid of the Second World War – a night

attacked and sank the German battleship *Tirpitz* moored in a Norwegian fjord near Tromso.

**1945** **12 March**: Bomber Command launched its largest raid on a single target during the whole of the Second World War when 1,108

attack by 107 Lancasters of No. 5 Group on an oil target at Vallo in southern Norway.

**1945** **2 May**: Operation Exodus began, with Lancasters conveying twenty-four ex-Prisoners of War in each aircraft from the Continent back to England.

**1945** **June**: The Lancaster VII entered service with No. 617 Squadron at RAF Waddington.

**1945** **4 June**: The British Chiefs of Staff accepted the American proposal for ten RAF Lancaster squadrons to be based in Okinawa.

**1945** **6 August**: Atomic bomb dropped on Hiroshima, Japan.

**1945** **9 August**: Atomic bomb dropped on Nagasaki, Japan.

**1945** **October**: The last Lancaster III

(TX273) was delivered from the Yeadon factory.

**1945** **10 December**: Trial lifeboat dropping began by No. 279 Squadron at RAF Thornaby. RF310/RL-A successfully dropped the first boat by parachute.

▲

*Lancaster I in the colours of 9 Squadron's W4964 when it took part in the 1944 Tirpitz raid in November 1944.*

**1946** **January**: Nos 617 and 9 Squadrons moved to India and saw action over the North-West Frontier.

**1946** **2 February**: The last Lancaster to enter RAF service was B.I(FE) TW910, delivered by Armstrong Whitworth.

**1946** **9 July–29 August**: Lancaster Is of No. 35 Squadron at RAF Graveley made a goodwill tour of the USA.

**1947** **23 August**: Roy Chadwick, the Lancaster's designer, was tragically killed on a test flight from Woodford in an Avro Tudor airliner, together with the company's chief test pilot, Bill Thorn.

**1950** **March**: The last Lancaster bomber squadron (No. 49) converted to Avro Lincolns.

**1950** **August**: Lancaster ASR3s and GR3s were declared obsolete.

**1953** **December**: The last Lancaster in Bomber Command, a PR.I (PA427), was retired.

**1954** **20 February**: The last Lancasters in overseas service with the RAF were the MR3s of No. 38 Squadron at Malta – the last (RF273) was flown back to England.

**1956** **15 October**: Retirement of the RAF's last Lancaster, an MR3, in service with the School of Maritime Reconnaissance at RAF St Mawgan.

**1964** **1 April**: The last three RCAF Lancasters were withdrawn from service, twenty-three years after the prototype's first flight.

**1965** **October**: Lancaster PA474 taken

on charge by the RAF's Historical Branch.

**1988**  **11 September**: One of the largest and most ambitious restoration projects ever undertaken in Canada came to fruition as the Mynarski Memorial Lancaster 'KB726'/C-GVRA lifted off the runway at Hamilton Airport and became airborne.

**1995/6**  **Winter**: PA474 received a new wing spar at RAF St Athan.

**2006/7**  **Winter**: PA474 was given a new Nos 100/550 Squadron *Phantom of the Ruhr* colour scheme at Coventry.

'Its efficiency was almost incredible, both in performance and in the way in which it could be saddled with ever-increasing loads without breaking the camel's back. It is astonishing that so small an aircraft as the Lancaster could take the 22,000lb Grand Slam bomb, a weapon which no other aircraft in the world could or yet can carry. The Lancaster far surpassed all other types of heavy bombers. Not only could it take heavier bomb loads, not only was it easier to handle and not only were there fewer accidents with this than any other types; throughout the war the casualty rate of Lancasters was also consistently below that of other types.'

Marshal of the Royal Air Force Sir Arthur T. Harris
Bt GCB, OBE, AFC, LLD,
Air Officer Commanding-in-Chief, Bomber Command
February 1942–September 1945.